"The best way to predict the future is to invent it."

— Alan Kay

To the dreamers, the doers, and the doubters.

To my beautiful wife and our two incredible daughters, who inspire me every day with their love and support.

To everyone with curiosity and hope—from children in remote villages to grandparents embracing technology, from busy parents to artists, teachers, entrepreneurs, coders, creators, and caregivers.

This book is for all who dare to imagine a better future and take action today, not someday.

May these stories show you that change is possible, that AI can serve humanity well, and that your role matters.

Wherever you are, this is your invitation to lead, learn, and lift others.

Preface

When I first began exploring artificial intelligence (AI), I was fascinated by the headlines—machines outsmarting grandmasters, algorithms diagnosing disease. But what truly moved me were the quieter stories. The ones where AI didn't just impress. It helped. It gave someone their time back. Their voice. Their freedom. Their spark.

This book is a collection of those stories.

100 Ways AI Can Change Your Life Today isn't about coding or computer science. It's about people like you—parents, teachers, artists, business owners, students, caregivers—who dared to ask: *What if this tool could help me?*

Some used AI to rebuild after disaster. Others launched businesses, supported loved ones, or transformed grief. They didn't all have technical backgrounds. What they had was curiosity. And courage. They weren't trying to build the next big thing—just a better day.

This book grounds you in reality. The *now.* AI is already doing extraordinary things in ordinary lives. And the only thing missing from these pages... is your story.

You'll meet parents, farmers, teenagers, engineers, artists—each using AI practically. My hope is that one story sparks a realization that you too can engage with this technology today.

Because you don't have to be an expert to take the first step.

You just have to start.

Introduction

Artificial intelligence (AI) is no longer the stuff of science fiction. It's not something that's coming—it's already here, woven quietly into the fabric of our daily lives. From the apps on your phone to the systems that power your home, from the tools reshaping how we work to the ones helping us care for our loved ones, AI is everywhere. But here's the surprising truth: most people have no idea how much power they already have at their fingertips.

This book is here to change that.

100 Ways AI Can Change Your Life Today is not about future speculation. It's not about robots taking over the world or complex theories meant for engineers. It's about everyday people—individuals from all walks of life—who are using AI right now to live smarter, freer, more creative, and more meaningful lives at work and in business. It's about a mother of two who built an AI app to ease the chaos of parenting. A psychologist who used AI to scale empathy through a chatbot. An engineer who designed a smart home that could one day save lives. And many more.

The 100 unique stories in these pages are grounded in action. They show what's possible when we stop fearing the unknown and start engaging with it—boldly, curiously, and intentionally. Some examples are big, others are small, but each one represents a spark of what can happen when people harness technology for good.

The goal of this book isn't to make you an expert in AI. It's to open your eyes to the many ways you can use it right now, in your own life, with your own goals. Whether you want to become more productive, solve a challenge, create something new, or simply understand what's going on in the world around you—this book is your invitation to step in and co-create with artificial intelligence.

Contents

Why This Book Matters - Right Now

Artificial Intelligence (AI) is no longer a futuristic fantasy. It's here, now, reshaping every corner of our world—and the pace of change is only accelerating. Whether you realize it or not, AI is already transforming how we live, learn, work, create, travel, and connect. The question is no longer *if* AI will affect your life. The question is: *Will you be an active participant in the change, or a passive observer left behind?*

This book is your invitation to step into the future—not by waiting for it to arrive, but by recognizing the dozens of ways it's already at your fingertips today.

You don't need to be a tech expert. You don't need a coding background. What you *do* need is curiosity, courage, and the willingness to engage with tools that are increasingly accessible, intuitive, and often free. Across these 100 case studies, you'll meet everyday people—parents, students, artists, teachers, solopreneurs, retirees—who are improving their lives and work with the help of AI. They aren't just riding the wave of innovation; they're shaping it.

From automating mundane tasks to unlocking creativity, from saving lives in hospitals to launching dream careers from kitchen tables, AI is empowering everyday individuals to do more, reach further, and think bigger.

Each story in this book is proof that you don't need to wait for permission to get started. You don't need to overhaul your life or business overnight. You just need to take one step—one tool, one use case, one idea—that can unlock a chain reaction of impact.

The urgency is real. But so is the opportunity.

These storied examples are not sequential and can be read in any order. While all unique in their own way, they share the common thread of embracing AI. By the time you finish this book, we hope you'll not only understand what AI can do—you'll believe in what *you* can do with AI.

Let's begin.

Everyday Life, Upgraded

"The simple things are also the most extraordinary things, and only the wise can see them." — Paulo Coelho

Artificial intelligence (AI) has seamlessly integrated into our daily lives, enhancing convenience, efficiency, and security. This section explores three detailed case studies demonstrating AI's transformative impact on everyday living.

1. The Smart Home That Saved a Family

The integration of AI into home automation has revolutionized residential living, offering enhanced security, energy efficiency, and personalized comfort. Families are increasingly adopting AI-driven smart home solutions to streamline daily routines and safeguard their households.

In Cairns, Queensland, engineer Julius Arnold-Janco has pioneered a groundbreaking smart home that seamlessly integrates advanced technology with compassionate healthcare design. Motivated by personal experiences—witnessing his grandfather's distressing hospital passing compared to his grandmother's peaceful end at home—Arnold-Janco envisioned a residence that offers dignified in-home medical care within a comforting environment.

Central to the home's design is a hospital-grade bedroom equipped with essential medical infrastructure, including air supply, oxygen, and Residual Current Device (RCD)-protected power circuits that comply with Australian healthcare standards. This setup facilitates various medical needs such as palliative care, wound management, and recovery from illnesses, enabling residents to receive professional medical attention without leaving their home.

Enhancing the home's functionality is "Cora," a bespoke, voice-controlled AI assistant. Cora manages security by monitoring cameras, detecting intruders, sounding alarms, and alerting neighbors when necessary. Beyond security, Cora is equipped with internal water leak and termite detection capabilities, proactively identifying potential maintenance issues. Notably, this AI system operates independently of external brand ecosystems or internet connections, ensuring user data remains secure within the home.

Constructed with resilience in mind, the house features 150mm thick walls, a 295mm thick slab roof, and triple-glazed glass, making it capable of withstanding cyclonic conditions. Despite its robust structure, the design does not compromise on aesthetics or environmental sustainability, incorporating luxury finishes and eco-friendly materials. The architectural design creates an illusion of the house "floating," blending modernity with functionality.

Arnold-Janco's innovative approach serves as a template for future housing, demonstrating how technology and thoughtful design can create homes that cater to both comfort and critical healthcare needs. By integrating AI and medical facilities into residential settings, this model addresses challenges in public healthcare systems and offers a dignified alternative for in-home medical care.

This Cairns smart home exemplifies the potential of combining advanced technology with empathetic design, paving the way for residences that are not only intelligent and secure but also responsive to the evolving healthcare needs of inhabitants.

The implementation of AI in this smart home has significantly improved the family's quality of life. The AI assistant's proactive monitoring has prevented potential hazards, ensuring the household's safety. Energy consumption has decreased due to intelligent climate control and lighting systems, leading to cost savings. The family's daily routines have become more efficient, allowing more time for personal activities and reducing stress. This case exemplifies how AI-driven smart home technology can create a safer, more comfortable, and energy-efficient living environment.

2. Parenting in the Digital Age: How Goldee Lightens the Load

Managing a household, coordinating family schedules, and balancing work responsibilities can be overwhelming for parents. The mental load of remembering appointments, school events, and daily tasks often leads to stress and burnout. AI personal assistants have emerged as valuable tools to help parents organize and manage their family's activities more efficiently.

Verity Tuck, an accomplished entrepreneur and mother of two, co-founded Goldee, an AI-powered personal assistant designed to alleviate the mental load associated with parenting. Her inspiration stemmed from personal experiences of being overwhelmed by the myriad tasks and communications involved in managing family life, especially after her daughter began school. Tuck observed that the influx of emails, WhatsApp messages, school newsletters, and event reminders became unmanageable, leading her to seek a technological solution to streamline these responsibilities.

Research indicates that women disproportionately bear the household's mental load, with studies showing they handle approximately 70% of family management tasks. This imbalance often results in burnout and stress among mothers. Recognizing this, Tuck aimed to create a tool that not only organizes tasks but also promotes equitable distribution of responsibilities among family members.

Goldee offers several functionalities tailored to support busy families:

- Integration with Communication Platforms: The app seamlessly connects with emails, WhatsApp, and other messaging services, allowing parents to forward information directly to Goldee. The AI then scans and extracts pertinent details, transforming them into organized tasks and events.

- Automated Scheduling and Reminders: Goldee creates a centralized family calendar, schedules appointments, sets reminders, and allocates tasks among family members. This ensures that everyone is informed and responsibilities are shared.

- Learning Family Routines: Over time, Goldee adapts to a family's unique routines, offering personalized assistance and timely notifications that align with established patterns.

Tuck and her husband, Mike Fraser, who is also a co-founder of Goldee, leveraged their entrepreneurial backgrounds and personal experiences to develop the app. They conducted pilot programs involving prototypes and collaborations with parents to validate their hypotheses on the challenges and needs of family management. The feedback from these pilots was instrumental in refining Goldee's features to ensure they effectively addressed the pain points of their target users.

Since its launch, Goldee has received positive feedback from users, with many parents reporting significant reductions in stress and improvements in family organization. The app has been recognized for its innovative approach to integrating AI into daily family life, offering a practical solution to the often-overwhelming mental load carried by parents.

Users of Goldee have reported saving an average of 4 hours per week, reducing stress and allowing more quality time with their families. The app's intuitive interface and proactive assistance have helped parents feel more in control of their schedules, leading to improved well-being. By automating routine organizational tasks, Goldee enables parents to focus on more meaningful interactions with their children, enhancing family dynamics. This case highlights the potential of AI personal assistants to transform family life by reducing the cognitive burden on parents.

3. From Code to Compassion: The Story Behind Woebot's Digital Therapy

Alison Darcy, a clinical research psychologist, recognized the global challenge of providing accessible mental health support. Traditional therapy often faced barriers such as cost, stigma, and availability, leaving many individuals without the help they needed. Determined to bridge this gap, Darcy envisioned leveraging technology to create an innovative solution.

In 2017, Darcy founded Woebot, an AI-powered chatbot designed to offer mental health support through conversational interactions. Woebot utilizes principles of cognitive behavioral therapy (CBT) to engage users in meaningful dialogues, helping them navigate emotional challenges and develop coping strategies. The chatbot is accessible via smartphones, providing users with immediate support regardless of time or location.

Woebot's design focuses on creating a relatable and empathetic user experience. Drawing inspiration from characters like Spock and Kermit the Frog, as well as her compassionate friend Eric Bayer, Darcy aimed to imbue Woebot with a personality that balances humor and care. This approach fosters a non-judgmental environment where users feel comfortable discussing their feelings.

Since its launch, Woebot has interacted with approximately 1.5 million people, offering support and evidence-based techniques to manage mental health issues. Research indicates that engaging with Woebot can lead to reductions in symptoms of depression and anxiety within two weeks, demonstrating its efficacy as a digital therapeutic tool.

Alison Darcy's development of Woebot exemplifies how artificial intelligence can be harnessed to address critical societal needs. By creating an accessible, engaging, and evidence-based platform, Darcy has expanded the reach of mental health support, offering a valuable resource to those who might otherwise go without assistance. Woebot stands as a testament to the potential of AI in enhancing well-being and transforming the landscape of mental health care.

Health & Wellness

"It is health that is real wealth and not pieces of gold and silver." — Mahatma Gandhi

Across industries, a quiet revolution is unfolding—reshaping how we heal, learn, and manage our finances. With enhanced efficiency, tailored experiences, and smarter decision-making, AI is the catalyst driving this transformation. In the pages ahead, we explore three inspiring case studies that highlight its powerful impact in healthcare, education, and finance—unveiling a future full of promise and potential.

4. Breathing Easier: The AI Revolution in COPD Management

John, a 68-year-old retired truck driver from Peoria, Illinois, had been managing chronic obstructive pulmonary disease (COPD) for nearly a decade. A smoker in his younger years, John had faced multiple hospitalizations in recent years due to sudden flare-ups of his condition—sometimes requiring emergency care. Each exacerbation left him weaker, more anxious, and fearful of another episode he might not survive.

His doctors tried everything—from medication adjustments to home oxygen—but traditional methods of managing COPD often meant reacting only *after* symptoms became severe. That cycle changed when John became part of a pilot program at OSF HealthCare that was using artificial intelligence to change how chronic conditions like his were managed.

OSF HealthCare had recently implemented a predictive analytics model that could identify patients at high risk for hospital readmission. This system didn't just rely on static data—it continuously analyzed a wide range of inputs from the hospital's electronic health records (EHR), including John's vital signs, lab test results, oxygen saturation levels, medication adherence, and even subtle indicators like changes in weight or pulse rate.

The AI model flagged John as "high risk" for another COPD exacerbation within 30 days of his last discharge—even though he felt relatively fine. The system had detected a combination of early indicators: slightly increasing inflammation markers, minor drops in oxygen, and a recent lapse in medication refill.

Thanks to the AI alert, John's care team quickly sprang into action. His physician scheduled a home visit with a respiratory therapist, who made small but crucial changes to his inhaler use. A nurse checked in daily via telehealth, monitoring his vitals remotely. Perhaps most importantly, John and his wife received tailored education about early warning signs and the importance of medication timing—something they hadn't fully understood before.

The early intervention worked. John avoided the emergency room entirely. Over the next 90 days, he didn't experience a single COPD-related hospitalization—the longest stretch he'd gone in years. His confidence grew, his quality of life improved, and his wife, Marlene, said it was "the first time we didn't feel like we were just waiting for the next ambulance ride."

John now sees the AI model not as a machine, but as a "guardian angel in the background" helping his care team stay one step ahead. "It's not about replacing doctors—it's about giving them a head start," he says.

5. Finding Her Voice: Sarah's Journey with Ada

Sarah, a 19-year-old student at Bolton College, struggled with traditional learning methods due to her dyslexia. She often found it challenging to keep up with the standard curriculum and felt disengaged from her studies.

Bolton College's AI-powered virtual assistant, Ada, has significantly enhanced the learning experience for students like Sarah by providing personalized, real-time support tailored to individual needs.

Ada is designed to offer immediate responses to student inquiries, functioning as a 24/7 digital assistant. Students can access Ada both on-campus and remotely via a mobile app, allowing them to receive timely information and support whenever needed. This accessibility ensures that students like Sarah can get answers to their questions outside of regular classroom hours, facilitating continuous learning and reducing delays in obtaining assistance.

Ada seamlessly integrates with Bolton College's existing learning management systems, such as Moodle. This integration allows Ada to provide contextualized support within the platforms that students regularly use for their studies. For instance, when Sarah is working on an assignment in Moodle, she can interact with Ada to clarify concepts, access additional resources, or receive guidance on the assignment requirements without leaving the platform.

Bolton College is committed to enhancing Ada's capabilities by incorporating advanced AI technologies, including generative AI and local large language models (LLLMs). These advancements aim to provide more accurate and context-aware responses, further personalizing the learning experience. Additionally, the college is exploring the development of a visual representation of Ada, allowing for voice interactions, which would make the assistant more accessible to students with varying needs and preferences.

Sarah's academic performance improved notably, with her grades increasing by an average of 15% across subjects. She expressed increased confidence and motivation in her studies, attributing her success to the customized support provided by the AI assistant.

6. AI Helps Save Emily's Life with Early Detection of Sepsis

Emily, a 42-year-old mother of three, had always been relatively healthy. But after undergoing a routine surgery, she began experiencing unusual fatigue, confusion, and chills. Initially attributing these symptoms to post-operative recovery, Emily delayed seeking medical attention—until her condition worsened rapidly.

She was rushed to the hospital and admitted with what appeared to be early-stage sepsis, a life-threatening condition that often progresses too quickly for traditional detection methods to intervene in time. But this time, technology changed the outcome.

At the hospital, Emily's vital signs were being monitored through an AI-powered clinical decision support system. This AI system constantly analyzed her real-time vitals—heart rate, oxygen levels, temperature, and blood pressure—against a vast dataset of previous sepsis cases. Within minutes, it flagged a high-risk pattern: an early but subtle combination of abnormalities that suggested sepsis could be developing.

An alert was immediately sent to the attending medical team. Based on the AI's early warning, they administered antibiotics and fluids well before typical symptoms had fully presented, giving Emily a head start in fighting the infection.

Thanks to the AI's timely prediction and the medical team's swift action, Emily avoided full septic shock. She recovered in the ICU over several days but walked out of the hospital with minimal long-term effects—something her doctors said would have been highly unlikely without early intervention.

For Emily, the experience was life-changing. "The nurses told me that without that system flagging the warning signs, I probably would have crashed within hours," she recalled. "It's strange to say, but AI might've saved my life."

Today, Emily is back to her normal routine—but with a renewed sense of gratitude and curiosity about the technologies quietly working in the background of modern medicine. Her story is one of many that shows how AI isn't just a futuristic tool—it's already transforming care, one life at a time.

Smarter Workflows

"Work smarter, not harder." — Allen F. Morgenstern

A quiet force is reshaping the way we work—streamlining tasks, sharpening decisions, and fueling productivity like never before. From empowering solopreneurs to enabling fairer hiring practices and transforming how we manage communication, intelligent tools are redefining business operations. This section dives into three powerful case studies that showcase how innovation is driving smarter, more human-centric ways to work and grow.

7. Solopreneur Automates Business Operations with AI

Solopreneurs often juggle multiple roles—from marketing to customer service—which can be overwhelming and limit business growth. The advent of AI-powered tools offers opportunities to automate routine tasks, allowing solopreneurs to focus on strategic initiatives.

Tom Kadala, founder of RagingFX.com, exemplifies the innovative potential of AI and cloud technologies in creating a "zero-employee autonomous company." Over the past seven years, Kadala has developed and refined a machine learning algorithm that autonomously manages both the deliverables and administrative functions of his business through agentic workflows. Operating entirely from the cloud, this AI-driven system handles tasks such as client communications, project management, and financial transactions without the need for human intervention.

In this setup, Kadala positions himself as essentially another client of his own business, overseeing the AI system and focusing on strategic business development rather than daily operations. This approach has allowed him to reduce overhead costs associated with hiring employees and maintaining physical office space. The efficiency of the AI system has also enabled faster project turnaround times and improved client satisfaction. Kadala's experience demonstrates how solopreneurs can harness AI to create scalable and efficient business models, redefining traditional notions of company structure and operations.

Kadala's innovative approach has garnered attention in the business community. In a letter to the Financial Times, he shared his experience of operating an autonomous company, highlighting the challenges and rewards of this business model. He noted that during social gatherings, he often encounters individuals who struggle to grasp the concept of an autonomous company, finding it mind-boggling while it feels perfectly normal to him.

The success of RagingFX.com underscores a broader trend where AI is enabling entrepreneurs to rethink traditional business structures. By automating routine tasks, solopreneurs can focus on strategic growth initiatives, leading to more agile and responsive businesses. This paradigm shift not only enhances efficiency but also opens new avenues for innovation and competitiveness in the market.

8. Breaking Bias: Kade's Journey to Fair Employment

Unconscious bias in recruitment can lead to a lack of diversity and missed opportunities for organizations. Artificial intelligence (AI) has the potential to mitigate these biases by focusing on candidates' qualifications and experiences rather than subjective factors.

Kade, a dedicated disability support worker, experienced firsthand the challenges of job hunting. The traditional process of searching through job listings, manually applying for roles, and crafting individualized cover letters was time-consuming and often discouraging. Kade's experience reflects a common struggle among job seekers, where the sheer volume of tasks can be overwhelming and inefficient.

Upon discovering Employment Hero's SmartMatch, Kade's approach to job searching transformed. By uploading his CV, SmartMatch automatically created a comprehensive candidate profile, highlighting his skills, experiences, and certifications. The AI-driven system then matched him with roles that aligned with his qualifications, eliminating the need for extensive manual searches. This streamlined process not only saved time but also ensured that Kade was considered for positions that truly fit his professional background.

SmartMatch's design focuses on evaluating candidates based on their competencies, deliberately removing identifiers such as gender, age, and visual cues. This approach aims to create a more equitable hiring process by preventing biases that can occur in traditional recruitment methods. For Kade, this meant that his application was assessed purely on merit, providing a fair opportunity to showcase his suitability for the role.

The impact of this unbiased, AI-driven recruitment process was significant. Kade secured a position with Bloomfield Support Solutions in a matter of days—a stark contrast to the often prolonged and uncertain timelines associated with conventional job searches. His success story underscores the potential of AI tools like SmartMatch to revolutionize recruitment by promoting diversity and inclusivity. By focusing solely on relevant qualifications and experiences, organizations can access a broader, more diverse talent pool, ultimately enhancing their workforce with individuals selected for their true capabilities.

Kade's experience exemplifies how thoughtful implementation of AI in recruitment can lead to more equitable outcomes for candidates and more effective hiring processes for organizations.

9. Empowering Project Management with Agentic AI Solutions

Lucy, a seasoned project manager at a mid-sized marketing firm, faced mounting challenges as her responsibilities expanded. Coordinating multiple campaigns, managing cross-functional teams, and ensuring timely deliverables became increasingly complex. Recognizing the need for a more efficient approach, Lucy explored technological solutions and discovered the potential of agentic workflows.

Agentic workflows involve AI-driven sequences of tasks that execute dynamically with minimal human intervention. Unlike traditional automation, these workflows utilize AI agents capable of perceiving their environment, making decisions within defined parameters, and taking appropriate actions.

Lucy implemented an agentic workflow system to streamline project management processes. The AI agents within this system autonomously handled task assignments, monitored project progress, and flagged potential bottlenecks. For instance, when a team member completed a task, the system automatically assigned the next step to the appropriate individual based on workload and expertise. If delays were detected, the AI agents proactively notified Lucy, suggesting corrective actions.

To achieve this, Lucy leveraged solutions from leading AI companies specializing in agentic workflows. She considered platforms like UiPath, known for transitioning from traditional robotic process automation to agentic AI, integrating deterministic software automation with non-deterministic AI capabilities like large language models. This integration allowed for more adaptive and intelligent automation processes.

Additionally, Lucy explored Aisera, which offers domain-specific, battle-tested AI agents designed to transform work and deliver business value. Aisera's platform provided autonomous execution, automating tasks and transforming workflows, which aligned with Lucy's goal of enhancing operational efficiency.

Another consideration was Beam AI, a platform that enables businesses to hire self-learning AI agents to run operations. Beam AI's agents operate continuously, reducing errors and increasing productivity, allowing businesses to scale without additional human resource costs.

The impact was immediate and significant. Project timelines improved as tasks were seamlessly transitioned between team members without manual oversight. Lucy found herself liberated from micromanaging daily operations, allowing her to focus on strategic planning and client engagement. The team's morale also received a boost, as clear task assignments and reduced administrative burdens fostered a more collaborative environment.

Lucy's experience underscores the transformative potential of agentic workflows in modern business settings. By integrating AI agents capable of autonomous decision-making and task execution, organizations can enhance efficiency, reduce operational bottlenecks, and empower employees to focus on higher-value activities. This case exemplifies how embracing advanced AI solutions from companies like UiPath, Aisera, and Beam AI can lead to tangible improvements in both productivity and workplace satisfaction.

Financial Freedom

"Do not save what is left after spending, but spend what is left after saving." — Warren Buffett

Money management is being redefined. Smarter investments, personalized budgeting, and powerful tools to detect fraud are no longer the domain of financial experts alone—they're becoming accessible to anyone with curiosity and a connection. In the stories ahead, you'll discover how individuals and institutions alike are using cutting-edge tools to grow wealth, protect assets, and take control of their financial futures—faster, safer, and more intelligently than ever before.

10. Revolutionizing Returns: The Impact of AI on Modern Investing

In the evolving landscape of investment management, professionals are increasingly turning to artificial intelligence (AI) to enhance efficiency and client engagement. A notable example is a wealth manager overseeing over $1 billion in assets under management (AUM), who integrated Boosted.ai's Alfa into his practice. This AI-driven platform enabled him to expand his stock coverage from 500 to 2,000 stocks per quarter while reducing research time by 60%. This significant improvement allowed for more personalized client interactions and informed investment strategies.

Similarly, individual investors are exploring AI tools to inform their decisions. An investing editor at Money.com conducted an experiment using Danelfin's AI-powered stock-picking tool. The platform recommended stocks like United Airlines (UAL) and Costco (COST), which were then compared against the S&P 500 index and a stock chosen by his 5-year-old son. Over 90 trading days, UAL, recommended by Danelfin, surged by over 90%, significantly outperforming the S&P 500's 7.79% increase. This outcome highlighted the potential of AI in identifying high-performing stocks.

These instances underscore the growing role of AI in investment management, offering tools that can process vast datasets to uncover insights and opportunities that might elude traditional analysis. While AI provides advanced analytics, financial experts emphasize that it should complement, not replace, human judgment. A diversified investment approach remains essential, with AI serving as a valuable component in a comprehensive strategy.

As AI technology continues to evolve, its integration into investment practices is poised to become more prevalent, offering both institutional and individual investors enhanced tools to navigate the complexities of the financial markets.

11. Streamlining Spending: BudgetBot's Role in Financial Wellness

Managing personal finances can be a daunting task, especially for individuals with demanding careers. Jane, a 34-year-old marketing executive, found herself struggling to keep track of her expenses and adhere to a budget. The manual effort required to record every transaction and categorize spending was overwhelming, leading to inconsistent tracking and a lack of clarity about her financial health.

Seeking a solution, Jane turned to BudgetBot, an AI-powered personal finance assistant developed by Freeport Metrics. BudgetBot offered a streamlined approach to financial management by allowing users to input expenditures through various means, including photographing receipts and verbal commands. The AI system would then categorize these expenses, providing organized data and insights into spending habits.

For Jane, this technology was transformative. She could simply snap a photo of a receipt or verbally log an expense, and BudgetBot would handle the rest. The AI's ability to recognize and categorize expenses accurately meant that Jane no longer had to spend hours manually inputting data. Over time, BudgetBot identified patterns in her spending behavior, offering tailored advice to help her achieve her financial goals. For instance, it alerted her to areas where she was overspending and suggested adjustments to her budget.

The app also featured interactive elements, such as gamified challenges and personalized recommendations, which engaged Jane and encouraged consistent use. This proactive approach not only made budgeting less tedious but also more effective. Jane reported an increased awareness of her spending patterns and found it easier to adhere to her budgeting plans. The real-time feedback and suggestions empowered her to adjust her spending behaviors proactively, leading to better financial outcomes.

Jane's experience with BudgetBot exemplifies how AI-driven tools can simplify financial management, making it more accessible and less daunting. By automating the tracking and categorization of expenses, such applications reduce the manual effort required in traditional budgeting, allowing users to focus on making informed financial decisions. This case highlights the potential of AI personal finance assistants to transform the way individuals manage their finances, leading to improved financial health and well-being.

12. Robo-Advisors Democratize Investment Management

In 2003, four visionaries—Alexander Fleiss, Jonathan Sturges, Jeremy Newton, and Spencer Greenberg—founded Rebellion Research, a New York-based investment management firm. Their mission was to harness artificial intelligence (AI) to revolutionize investment strategies. By 2006, they launched one of Wall Street's first AI-only funds, pioneering the integration of machine learning in asset management.

Central to Rebellion Research's approach is its proprietary AI system, "Star." Utilizing Bayesian networks, Star analyzes a vast array of data—from macroeconomic indicators across 53 countries to individual stock prices—to predict market trends. Each morning, Star generates a list of investment recommendations, which human traders review and execute. This synergy between AI-driven insights and human judgment allows for data-informed decisions while retaining essential oversight.

The efficacy of this AI-driven strategy became evident during the 2008 financial crisis. While many traditional funds struggled, Rebellion Research's AI system successfully navigated the tumultuous market, showcasing the potential of machine learning in identifying opportunities and managing risks during unprecedented times.

Rebellion Research's success has not only demonstrated the viability of AI in investment management but has also paved the way for broader acceptance of AI-driven strategies in the financial sector. By continuously refining their algorithms and expanding their data analysis capabilities, they exemplify how technology can enhance investment decision-making, making sophisticated strategies more accessible to a wider range of investors.

Entrepreneurs Empowered

"Success usually comes to those who are too busy to be looking for it." — Henry David Thoreau

A new era of entrepreneurship is unfolding—one where bold ideas meet intelligent technology. With powerful tools that elevate branding, sharpen marketing strategies, and transform customer service, AI is becoming a game-changer for visionary entrepreneurs. In this section, we uncover three inspiring case studies that reveal how today's innovators are using AI to launch, grow, and thrive like never before.

13. Designing Success: How AI Empowered a Blogger's Brand Identity

Establishing a strong brand identity is crucial for startups, yet many entrepreneurs face challenges due to limited budgets and design expertise. Traditionally, creating a professional logo required hiring graphic designers, which could be costly and time-consuming. The emergence of AI-powered logo generators has democratized the branding process, enabling startups to develop unique and professional logos efficiently.

Amit, a freelance writer and blogger specializing in digital marketing and online entrepreneurship, recognized the need for a distinctive logo to elevate his blog's professional appeal. Lacking design expertise and operating on a limited budget, Amit sought an efficient solution to create a unique visual identity. He turned to LogoAi.com, an AI-powered logo generator renowned for its user-friendly interface and customization capabilities. By inputting his blog's name, industry, and style preferences, Amit received a variety of tailored logo options. After selecting and refining a design that resonated with his brand vision, he implemented the new logo across his blog and social media platforms. The result was a significant increase in brand recognition and audience engagement, demonstrating how AI-driven tools can empower individuals to establish compelling brand identities without the need for extensive design skills or financial investment

The adoption of AI logo generators has significantly benefited startups by reducing the time and cost associated with developing a brand identity. Entrepreneurs can quickly produce high-quality logos that resonate with their target audience, facilitating a strong market presence from the outset. Additionally, the accessibility of these tools empowers startups to maintain consistency across various branding materials, enhancing overall brand recognition and credibility.

14. Precision Marketing: Leveraging AI for Unprecedented Growth

In the competitive world of e-commerce, effective advertising is crucial for driving traffic and increasing sales. Traditional advertising methods often rely on broad targeting and manual adjustments, which may not yield optimal results. The emergence of AI-powered advertising platforms has revolutionized this landscape by offering data-driven insights and automation, enabling businesses to optimize their marketing campaigns more effectively.

Consider the experience of 2X Monster Trucks, a company specializing in organizing monster truck events. The company faced challenges in scaling ad production across various events due to a lack of image variety, persona-specific visuals, and a clear strategy to boost Return on Ad Spend (ROAS) without overspending or relying on guesswork. To address these issues, 2X Monster Trucks partnered with Omneky, an AI-powered advertising platform. Omneky's technology generated tailored assets, scaled ad variations, and provided data-driven insights to guide high-performing creative with AI-powered precision. This collaboration resulted in 684 purchases and over $53,000 in revenue, while improving ROAS and cutting costs.

Similarly, GoSun, a company specializing in solar-powered appliances, sought to enhance its e-commerce sales through AI-driven advertising strategies. By leveraging Omneky's generative AI tools, GoSun achieved a 10% incremental lift, with ads accounting for 20% of total sales volume. The AI-powered platform enabled GoSun to uncover insights across multiple digital platforms, optimizing their advertising efforts and boosting overall sales.

These examples underscore the transformative impact of AI in e-commerce advertising. By automating the optimization of ad placements, content, and targeting parameters, businesses can deliver personalized and relevant advertisements to potential customers, thereby increasing engagement and conversion rates. The integration of AI not only enhances campaign performance but also allows marketing teams to focus on strategic planning and creative development, ultimately driving growth and improving return on investment.

15. AI-Powered Chatbots Transform Customer Service Operations

In the hospitality industry, delivering exceptional customer service is paramount. However, scaling support operations to meet increasing guest demands can be challenging and resource-intensive. To address this, Thon Hotels, a prominent hotel chain, integrated an AI-powered chatbot into their customer service framework, aiming to enhance efficiency and guest satisfaction.

Thon Hotels collaborated with AI specialists to develop a chatbot capable of handling a wide range of guest inquiries. Accessible through the hotel's website and mobile app, the chatbot was designed to provide immediate assistance on topics such as room availability, booking confirmations, check-in and check-out times, and information about hotel amenities. By leveraging natural language processing, the chatbot could engage in meaningful conversations, accurately interpret guest requests, and deliver relevant information promptly.

Understanding the importance of human touch in hospitality, Thon Hotels ensured that the chatbot was integrated seamlessly with their human support team. For complex or sensitive issues beyond the chatbot's capabilities, interactions were smoothly transferred to human agents. This hybrid approach allowed the hotel to maintain high-quality service while efficiently managing a large volume of inquiries.

The introduction of the AI chatbot led to significant improvements in Thon Hotels' customer service operations:

- Reduced Response Times: Guests received instant responses to common queries, enhancing their overall experience.
- Operational Efficiency: Automating routine interactions allowed human agents to focus on more complex tasks, optimizing resource allocation.
- Increased Guest Satisfaction: The combination of quick automated responses and accessible human support resulted in higher satisfaction levels among guests.

Thon Hotels' successful integration of an AI-powered chatbot exemplifies how the hospitality industry can leverage technology to enhance customer service. By thoughtfully combining AI capabilities with human expertise, businesses can achieve greater efficiency and elevate the guest experience.

Creatives & Artists

"Creativity is intelligence having fun." — Albert Einstein

A creative renaissance is underway—fueled by technology that amplifies imagination and expands what's possible. From writing stories to crafting visuals and producing cinematic masterpieces, creators are harnessing powerful tools to redefine the boundaries of art. This section showcases three captivating case studies that reveal how innovation is transforming the work of authors, artists, and filmmakers—unlocking new realms of expression and storytelling.

16. The Algorithmic Muse: How AI Shaped a New Literary Frontier

Mauro Javier Cárdenas, an acclaimed Ecuadorian-American author, has innovatively integrated artificial intelligence (AI) into his writing process, notably in his novel *American Abductions*. This collaboration between human creativity and machine learning has opened new avenues in literary composition.

In *American Abductions*, Cárdenas envisioned a character's car that converses in the distinctive style of surrealist writer Leonora Carrington. To authentically capture this, he developed a Natural Language Processing (NLP) model trained on Carrington's works. With permission from the Carrington estate, Cárdenas fed her writings into the AI system, enabling it to generate prose mirroring her unique voice. This AI-generated dialogue was then incorporated into the novel, enriching its narrative texture.

The AI's contributions introduced unexpected elements into the story, allowing Cárdenas to explore diverse narrative possibilities and character developments beyond his initial conceptions. This symbiotic relationship between author and AI facilitated a unique storytelling approach, blending traditional writing methodologies with technological innovation.

American Abductions received critical acclaim for its innovative narrative structure and depth. Cárdenas observed that the AI's involvement challenged conventional writing practices, suggesting that such tools can serve as catalysts for literary experimentation. He views AI as an opportunity for authors to expand their craft, emphasizing that these technologies can inspire greater novelty in literature.

Cárdenas's ethical approach to using AI—securing permissions and ensuring the responsible use of source material—sets a precedent in the literary community. His experience highlights the importance of thoughtful integration of AI in creative processes, respecting intellectual property while embracing technological advancements.

Mauro Javier Cárdenas's pioneering use of AI in *American Abductions* exemplifies the potential of machine learning as a co-creative tool in literature, offering authors new perspectives and expanding the horizons of storytelling

17. AI-Generated Art Achieves Commercial Success

The art world has undergone a transformative shift with the emergence of AI-generated artworks, challenging traditional notions of creativity and authorship. A prominent example of this evolution is Botto, an autonomous AI artist conceptualized by German artist Mario Klingemann and the software collective ElevenYellow in 2021.

Botto was designed as a decentralized autonomous artist capable of creating unique artworks through machine learning algorithms. Operating independently, Botto generates thousands of images weekly, exploring various themes and styles. These creations are then presented to a community known as BottoDAO—a decentralized autonomous organization comprising over 15,000 members—who vote on the most compelling pieces. The selected artworks are minted as NFTs (Non-Fungible Tokens) and auctioned in the digital art market.

The collaborative process between Botto and its community ensures that the AI's creations resonate with human aesthetic sensibilities. Each week, Botto proposes new thematic motifs for its "periods," marking different intervals of its artistic production. The community's feedback influences Botto's evolving style, creating a dynamic interplay between machine-generated art and human curation.

Since its inception, Botto has achieved significant milestones in the art market. By October 2024, Botto amassed over $4 million in total sales across 140 pieces, cementing its place in both digital and traditional art markets. Notably, in October 2024, Botto's solo exhibition at Sotheby's, titled "Exorbitant Stage: Botto, a Decentralized AI Artist," featured six artworks and garnered more than $350,000 in sales.

Beyond its artistic achievements, Botto is undergoing continuous evolution. Plans are underway to integrate a modified version of Mistral's open-source large language model, enabling Botto to converse about its artwork and develop a distinct personality. This enhancement aims to allow Botto to steer its creative direction more autonomously, potentially utilizing unaligned image generators to explore new artistic expressions.

Botto's success underscores the growing acceptance and value of AI-generated art in the mainstream art market. It exemplifies the evolving relationship between human artists and AI, suggesting a future where collaborative creation becomes more prevalent. By challenging traditional concepts of authorship and creativity, Botto invites a reexamination of what it means to be an artist in the digital age.

In summary, Botto represents a pioneering fusion of artificial intelligence and human collaboration, pushing the boundaries of contemporary art and opening new avenues for creative expression.

18. Filmmaker Utilizes AI for Solo Movie Editing

The filmmaking industry is undergoing a significant transformation with the integration of artificial intelligence (AI) tools, enabling solo creators to tackle complex tasks that traditionally required large teams. This democratization of technology allows independent filmmakers to produce high-quality content with reduced resources.

Chris, a seasoned video editor and motion graphic designer based in Dallas/Fort Worth, Texas, embarked on an innovative journey to incorporate AI into his video production process. Motivated by a curiosity about AI's potential in filmmaking, Chris initiated a project to explore how generative AI could assist in creating a commercial. His goal was to understand the capabilities and limitations of AI tools in a real-world production environment.

In his exploration, Chris employed various AI-powered tools to assist in different stages of production:

- Scriptwriting: He used AI to generate script ideas and dialogue, providing a foundation that he could refine and adapt to align with the project's vision.

- Storyboarding: AI applications helped create visual representations of scenes, enabling a clearer visualization of the narrative flow.

- Video Editing: Chris leveraged AI-driven editing software to automate repetitive tasks, such as sorting and tagging footage, allowing him to focus more on creative decision-making.

By inputting specific prompts and parameters, Chris guided the AI to produce content that resonated with his creative objectives. This collaboration between human intuition and machine efficiency streamlined the production process.

The project culminated in a commercial completed in a fraction of the time typically required. Chris observed that while AI tools significantly enhanced efficiency by handling technical aspects, the human touch remained essential in guiding the creative direction and ensuring the final product resonated with audiences. He emphasized that AI serves as an assistive technology, augmenting the filmmaker's capabilities rather than replacing them.

Chris' experience underscores the potential of AI to empower independent filmmakers, making high-quality production more accessible and cost-effective. By automating routine tasks, AI allows creators to allocate more time to artistic elements, fostering innovation and creativity in storytelling. As AI technology continues to evolve, it is poised to become an integral part of the filmmaking toolkit, offering new possibilities for solo creators and small production teams.

In conclusion, the integration of AI in filmmaking, as demonstrated by Chris, highlights a paradigm shift in content creation. It exemplifies how technology can be harnessed to enhance creative processes, enabling filmmakers to achieve professional-grade results with greater efficiency and flexibility.

Storytelling & Media

"Stories are the communal currency of humanity." — Tahir Shah

Storytelling and media are entering a bold new chapter—where creativity meets cutting-edge technology to unlock possibilities once confined to imagination. From co-writing with digital collaborators to reviving the voices of iconic actors and transforming podcast production, innovation is reshaping how stories are told and shared. This section delves into three compelling case studies that reveal the profound impact of intelligent tools on the future of narrative and media creation.

19. Alice and Sparkle: A Weekend Tale of AI and Imagination

In December 2022, Ammaar, a product-design manager based in San Francisco, embarked on an ambitious project to create a children's book using artificial intelligence (AI). Inspired during a bedtime story session with his friend's daughter, Ammaar aimed to craft a unique narrative despite lacking experience in creative writing and illustration.

Leveraging OpenAI's ChatGPT, Ammaar developed the storyline for "Alice and Sparkle," which follows a young girl named Alice who delves into the world of technology and creates her own AI companion, Sparkle. To bring the story to life visually, he employed Midjourney, an AI art generator, to produce illustrations that complemented the narrative. Remarkably, Ammaar completed the entire process—writing, illustrating, and self-publishing—within a span of 72 hours, making the book available on Amazon's digital bookstore.

The publication of "Alice and Sparkle" ignited a significant debate within the artistic and literary communities. While some praised the innovative use of AI in creative endeavors, many artists and writers expressed concerns about the ethical implications.

Critics argued that AI art generators, such as Midjourney, are trained on existing artworks without explicit consent from the original creators, raising issues of intellectual property rights and potential exploitation of artists' work.

Ammaar acknowledged these concerns, emphasizing the need for responsible development and use of AI tools. He advocated for involving artists in the creation process of AI technologies to ensure their rights and contributions are respected. Despite the backlash, Ammaar's project highlighted the evolving intersection of technology and creativity, underscoring the potential of AI to democratize content creation while also prompting critical discussions about its ethical use.

"Alice and Sparkle" serves as a case study in the transformative capabilities of AI in the creative industry, illustrating both the opportunities for innovation and the imperative for ethical considerations in the integration of technology and art.

20. AI Voice Clones Allow Late Actors to 'Return'

The entertainment industry has long sought ways to honor and preserve the legacies of iconic actors. With advancements in AI-driven voice cloning technology, it has become possible to recreate the voices of deceased actors, enabling their participation in new projects and offering audiences a nostalgic experience.

In 2024, the production team behind a documentary about the late actor Tommy Muñiz aimed to incorporate his voice into the film. They partnered with Respeecher, a company specializing in voice cloning technology. Using archival recordings of Muñiz, Respeecher's AI algorithms analyzed and synthesized his vocal patterns to create a digital voice model. This model was then used to generate new dialogue, allowing Muñiz's voice to narrate portions of the documentary. The process involved meticulous attention to detail to ensure the cloned voice authentically represented Muñiz's tone and inflection.

The documentary's release was met with acclaim, with audiences expressing appreciation for the authentic inclusion of Muñiz's voice. The use of AI voice cloning sparked discussions about the ethical implications and potential applications of such technology in the entertainment industry. While some voiced concerns about consent and the potential misuse of voice cloning, others highlighted its capacity to preserve artistic legacies and offer new creative possibilities. This case underscored the importance of establishing ethical guidelines and obtaining appropriate permissions when utilizing AI to recreate the likenesses of deceased individuals.

21. Family Rockets to Stardom with AI-Powered Kids' Podcast

Podcasting has become an increasingly popular medium for storytelling and information sharing. However, the production process can be labor-intensive, involving tasks such as transcription, editing, and content organization. Artificial intelligence (AI) tools have been developed to streamline these processes, enabling creators to produce high-quality content more efficiently.

A notable example of leveraging AI in podcast production is the "Out of This World – Stories for Kids" podcast, created by the VanderMolen family from Manistee County. Darin VanderMolen, an audio engineer and songwriter, was inspired to develop a children's podcast that combined quality production with engaging storytelling. To achieve this, the family integrated AI tools into various stages of their production process.

The VanderMolen family employed AI-driven transcription services to quickly convert recordings into text, facilitating easier editing and content refinement. Additionally, they utilized AI-based audio editing software to remove background noise and enhance sound quality, reducing the time spent on manual adjustments. For content creation, the family used AI to generate story ideas and scripts, which were then personalized and refined to ensure originality and emotional resonance.

The adoption of AI tools led to a significant reduction in production time, allowing the VanderMolen family to release episodes more frequently without compromising quality. Listeners responded positively to the improved audio clarity and engaging content, resulting in increased audience growth and retention. The streamlined workflow also provided the family with more creative freedom, enabling them to experiment with new formats and topics.

This case exemplifies how AI can enhance the efficiency and quality of podcast production, empowering creators to focus more on content and audience engagement. By automating routine tasks, AI allows independent podcasters to allocate more time to creative aspects, fostering innovation in their storytelling. As AI technology continues to evolve, it is poised to become an integral part of the podcasting toolkit, offering new possibilities for creators to produce compelling content with greater ease.

In conclusion, the VanderMolen family's experience with "Out of This World – Stories for Kids" demonstrates the transformative potential of AI in podcast production. By embracing AI tools, they have set a precedent for other independent creators seeking to enhance their production processes and deliver high-quality content to their audiences.

AI in the Kitchen

"Cooking is one of the strongest ceremonies for life." — Laura Esquivel

In modern kitchens, technology is revolutionizing the way we approach meal planning and food management. Innovative solutions are now offering personalized meal suggestions, efficient recipe recommendations, and strategies to minimize food waste. This section delves into three comprehensive case studies that highlight the significant impact of these advancements in transforming our culinary experiences.

22. From Pantry to Plate: How Smart Tech Helped Sarah Master Mealtime

Balancing a healthy diet with the constraints of a busy lifestyle and a limited pantry can be daunting. For individuals like Sarah, a graduate student juggling academic responsibilities and a tight budget, meal planning often felt overwhelming. The challenge of aligning nutritional goals with available ingredients led to repetitive meals and frequent food waste.

Seeking a solution, Sarah discovered the Simple Meals and Recipes Tonight (SMaRT) Pantry system, developed by researchers at the University of Chicago. This innovative tool utilizes machine learning to provide personalized recipe suggestions based on users' pantry contents, flavor preferences, cooking skills, and time constraints. By inputting her available ingredients and dietary preferences, Sarah received tailored meal options that not only matched her health objectives but also made efficient use of her existing food supplies.

The impact was immediate. Sarah found herself exploring new recipes, reducing food waste, and enjoying meals that aligned with her nutritional goals. The system's step-by-step instructions catered to her culinary skill level, making cooking a more enjoyable and less time-consuming task. Moreover, by minimizing the need for frequent grocery shopping, she managed to stay within her budget without compromising on meal quality.

Sarah's experience with SMaRT Pantry exemplifies how technology can empower individuals to make healthier food choices, optimize pantry usage, and transform meal preparation into a more manageable and satisfying part of daily life. By leveraging such tools, users can overcome common barriers to healthy eating, leading to improved well-being and reduced food waste.

23. AI Meal Planner Saves Busy Moms 10 Hours a Week

Balancing family meals with a hectic schedule is a challenge many parents face. Jessica Bonhoff, a mother of two and in-home daycare provider, found herself in this exact situation. Seeking a solution, she turned to AI-powered tools to streamline her meal planning process.

Jessica began using ChatGPT to assist with meal planning. By inputting her family's dietary preferences and available ingredients, she received tailored meal suggestions and organized shopping lists. This approach not only saved her time but also reduced food waste by utilizing items already in her pantry. Jessica noted, "We have leftover ciabatta rolls, so I can get a recipe including ciabatta rolls" .

The benefits extended beyond meal planning. Jessica reported that her grocery shopping became more efficient, staying within budget and minimizing unnecessary purchases. She also used AI to generate craft ideas for her daycare and even created a seven-day workout plan using equipment she had at home. As she put it, "As long as it's making her life easier, there is no going back" .

Jessica's experience highlights how integrating AI into daily routines can alleviate the stress of meal planning and enhance overall household management. By leveraging technology, busy parents can find more time to focus on what truly matters—spending quality time with their families.

24. From Code to Calories: The Teen Innovator Behind a $30M App

At just 18 years old, Zach Yadegari has emerged as a prominent figure in the tech industry, co-founding Cal AI, a groundbreaking nutrition tracking app that has garnered over 5 million downloads and achieved an impressive $30 million in annual recurring revenue within its first year.

Zach's journey into entrepreneurship began early. Before Cal AI, he successfully developed and sold a web gaming company for $100,000 . This initial venture laid the foundation for his future endeavors, showcasing his ability to identify market opportunities and execute innovative solutions.

Launched in May 2024, Cal AI revolutionized the way users approach nutrition tracking. By allowing individuals to simply photograph their meals, the app employs advanced image recognition and AI models from Anthropic and OpenAI to estimate calorie and macronutrient content with approximately 90% accuracy. This user-friendly approach addresses the common issue of manual data entry, making health tracking more accessible and less time-consuming.

Despite facing the typical challenges of startup development, including refining AI accuracy and ensuring user engagement, Zach and his team focused on creating a seamless user experience. Their efforts paid off, with Cal AI maintaining a 4.8-star rating on both the Apple App Store and Google Play, supported by tens of thousands of positive reviews .

In a surprising turn, Zach's applications to several top-tier universities, including Harvard, Yale, and Stanford, were rejected despite his 4.0 GPA and a 34 ACT score . This sparked widespread discussion on social media platforms, with many questioning the traditional metrics of academic success and the value placed on entrepreneurial achievements in college admissions.

Zach Yadegari's story is a testament to the impact of innovation, resilience, and the evolving landscape of success. As he continues to develop Cal AI and explore new ventures, his journey serves as an inspiration to aspiring entrepreneurs and a reminder that unconventional paths can lead to remarkable achievements.

Education Reimagined

"Tell me and I forget. Teach me and I remember. Involve me and I learn." — Benjamin Franklin

Artificial intelligence is transforming education by enabling personalized learning experiences that cater to diverse student needs. This chapter presents three real-life case studies demonstrating how individuals have harnessed AI to enhance educational outcomes. From AI-powered tutoring systems supporting students in underserved communities to educators streamlining administrative tasks, these examples highlight the profound impact of intelligent tools on the future of learning.

25. AI Tutoring Boosts Student Performance in Underserved Schools

In the heart of Ghana, a transformative educational initiative unfolded, addressing the challenges faced by students in underserved communities. Recognizing the limitations of traditional classroom settings—such as large class sizes and limited resources—educators sought innovative solutions to bridge the achievement gap.

Enter Rori, an AI-powered conversational math tutor accessible via WhatsApp. Developed by Rising Academies, Rori was introduced to support students in grades 3 through 9 across 11 schools. The program was designed to provide personalized math instruction tailored to each student's learning pace and needs. Students engaged with Rori for two 30-minute sessions per week over eight months, supplementing their regular math instruction.

Rori's interactive dialogues explained mathematical concepts, offered practice problems, and provided instant feedback, creating an engaging and adaptive learning environment. Notably, Rori was designed to operate on basic mobile devices and low-bandwidth networks, making it a scalable solution for other low- and middle-income countries facing similar challenges.

The impact of Rori was significant. Students who participated in the program demonstrated a substantial improvement in math performance, with an effect size of 0.36—equivalent to an additional year of learning. This outcome highlights the potential of AI-driven tutoring to enhance educational outcomes in resource-constrained settings.

Beyond academic gains, Rori also addressed students' emotional and psychological barriers to learning. By incorporating elements that promote a growth mindset and resilience, Rori helped students overcome math anxiety and build confidence in their abilities. This holistic approach to education underscores the importance of addressing both cognitive and emotional aspects of learning.

The success of Rori in Ghana serves as a compelling case study for the integration of AI in education. It demonstrates how technology can be harnessed to provide equitable learning opportunities, particularly in underserved communities. As educational institutions worldwide grapple with similar challenges, Rori offers a blueprint for leveraging AI to support and enhance student learning outcomes.

26. Empowering Educators: How AI Tools Transformed Amanda's Teaching Experience

High school science teacher Amanda faced the perennial challenge of balancing instructional time with administrative tasks. Grading assignments, crafting assessments, and providing individualized feedback often encroached upon the time she could spend engaging directly with her students.

Seeking a solution, Amanda integrated generative AI tools into her daily workflow. Utilizing platforms like ChatGPT, Brisk Teaching, Quizizz, and EdPuzzle, she streamlined the creation of multiple-choice questions and quizzes. Previously, assembling a test could take up to ten hours; with AI assistance, this process was reduced to approximately 40 minutes. These tools allowed her to input exam topics and generate diverse question sets, even enabling the creation of varied versions to prevent academic dishonesty.

Grading, particularly of short-answer questions, also became more efficient. AI provided initial feedback, which Amanda then personalized with specific comments on students' strengths and areas for improvement. This approach ensured consistency and timeliness in feedback, enhancing the learning experience for her students.

To further enhance classroom interaction, Amanda employed Merlyn Mind, an AI-powered voice assistant. This technology allowed her to control her computer screen remotely, enabling her to move freely around the classroom and engage more directly with students. For instance, during a dissection lab, when a student inquired about the body temperature of a chicken, Amanda could promptly provide an answer without breaking the flow of the lesson.

The integration of these AI tools led to significant time savings and reduced the risk of teacher burnout. Amanda could dedicate more time to direct instruction and student support, fostering a more interactive and responsive learning environment. Her experience exemplifies how embracing technological innovations can alleviate administrative burdens, allowing educators to focus on delivering high-quality, personalized education.

27. From Struggle to Speech: Transforming Dyslexia into Innovation

Cliff's journey from a young boy struggling with dyslexia to the founder of a revolutionary text-to-speech application exemplifies the transformative power of personal experience and technological innovation.

Diagnosed with dyslexia in the third grade, Cliff faced significant hurdles in reading and comprehension. He often found himself pretending to read, using coping mechanisms to mask his difficulties. The turning point came when his mother, after extensive research, identified his condition, leading to a diagnosis that brought clarity and relief. Listening to his father read "Harry Potter" aloud became a cherished experience, igniting his love for stories and highlighting the potential of auditory learning.

While attending Brown University, Cliff sought a solution to his reading challenges. He developed the initial version of Speechify, a text-to-speech application designed to convert written content into spoken words. Utilizing optical character recognition (OCR) and natural-sounding voices, Speechify allowed users to listen to books, articles, and documents, tailoring the experience to individual preferences. This innovation not only addressed his personal needs but also resonated with a broader audience facing similar challenges.

Speechify's user-friendly interface and effective functionality led to widespread adoption, with millions of users benefiting from its features. The application has been particularly impactful for individuals with dyslexia, ADHD, and other learning differences, enhancing accessibility and promoting independence in reading. Cliff's efforts earned him a spot on Forbes' 30 Under 30 list, acknowledging his contribution to making information more accessible.

Beyond the application, Cliffhas become an advocate for individuals with learning differences, sharing his story to inspire and educate others. Speechify continues to evolve, integrating new features and expanding its reach, embodying Cliff's commitment to leveraging technology to empower users worldwide.

Cliff's narrative underscores the potential of turning personal adversity into a catalyst for innovation, demonstrating how technology can bridge gaps and foster inclusivity in education and beyond

Smart Shopping & Style

"Fashion is about something that comes from within you." — Ralph Lauren

The fusion of technology and creativity is ushering in a transformative era in the shopping and fashion industries. Innovations are redefining online shopping experiences, enhancing accessibility for visually impaired individuals, and offering personalized skincare solutions. This section delves into three compelling case studies that showcase the profound impact of these advancements, illustrating how imagination and cutting-edge technology converge to revolutionize our interaction with fashion and retail.

28. Doji: Redefining Online Shopping with AI-Powered Virtual Fitting Rooms

In the ever-evolving landscape of online fashion retail, the challenge of replicating the tactile, in-store fitting experience has long plagued both consumers and retailers. High return rates and customer dissatisfaction due to sizing and style discrepancies have been persistent issues. Enter Doji, an AI-powered fashion app launched in 2024, aiming to bridge this gap by offering users the ability to create personalized avatars for virtual try-ons.

Doji's innovative approach allows users to upload multiple selfies and full-body images, enabling the app's advanced AI algorithms to generate a virtual model that closely resembles them. This personalized avatar can then try on curated designer clothing or imported items with shoppable links, providing a realistic preview of how garments would look and fit. By considering factors like fit, style, and fabric drape, Doji enhances the online shopping experience, making it more akin to in-store browsing.

The app's private beta phase garnered significant attention, with early users praising its accuracy and user-friendly interface. Notably, Reddit cofounder Alexis Ohanian's venture capital firm, Seven Seven Six, invested in Doji, highlighting the tech community's confidence in its potential. The app's ability to reduce uncertainty in online shopping aims to decrease return rates and improve overall customer satisfaction.

Doji's success underscores the transformative impact of AI in fashion e-commerce, offering a glimpse into a future where virtual try-ons become a standard feature, enhancing personalization and reducing the friction traditionally associated with online clothing purchases.

29. AI Assists Visually Impaired Individuals in Independent Shopping

Navigating the world without sight presents daily challenges, from finding a seat in a crowded café to selecting the right cereal box in a bustling grocery aisle. Recognizing these hurdles, engineers at the University of Colorado Boulder have developed a groundbreaking assistive device: a "smart" walking stick designed to empower visually impaired individuals with greater independence.

This innovative cane integrates a camera and computer vision technology to map and interpret the user's surroundings in real-time. By providing tactile feedback through handle vibrations and auditory cues like "reach a little bit to your right," the device guides users through complex environments. In laboratory tests simulating real-world settings, participants successfully located desired seats in 10 out of 12 trials, demonstrating the cane's potential to facilitate social interactions and personal autonomy.

Beyond seating navigation, the smart cane has been adapted for tasks like grocery shopping. In a mock store setup, users employed the cane to identify specific products on shelves, receiving precise instructions to locate and grasp items. This functionality not only enhances the shopping experience but also reduces reliance on assistance, fostering a sense of self-reliance.

The development team envisions a future iteration of the cane that operates via a standard smartphone, making the technology more accessible and portable. By transforming a traditional mobility aid into a sophisticated navigational tool, this smart walking stick exemplifies how technology can bridge gaps in accessibility, offering visually impaired individuals a greater degree of freedom and confidence in their daily lives.

30. Emma's Glow-Up: How AI Transformed Her Skincare Journey

Emma, a 34-year-old marketing professional from Chicago, had long struggled to find a skincare routine that addressed her specific concerns. Despite trying numerous products, she often felt overwhelmed by the vast array of options and uncertain about what would truly work for her skin type.

One evening, while browsing online, Emma discovered RoC Skincare's AI Skin Insight™ tool. Intrigued by the promise of personalized recommendations, she decided to give it a try. The process was straightforward: she uploaded a selfie and answered a brief questionnaire about her skin concerns and preferences. In under two minutes, the AI analyzed her skin, considering factors like texture, pigmentation, and fine lines. It then provided her with a customized AM and PM skincare regimen tailored to her unique needs.

Emma was impressed by the specificity of the recommendations. The regimen included products formulated to address her concerns about early signs of aging and uneven skin tone. Trusting the personalized approach, she decided to follow the suggested routine.

Over the next few weeks, Emma noticed significant improvements. Her skin appeared more radiant and even-toned, and the fine lines she had been concerned about seemed less pronounced. The tailored routine not only simplified her skincare process but also boosted her confidence, knowing she was using products suited to her individual needs.

Emma's experience reflects a broader trend in the skincare industry, where AI-driven personalization is transforming how consumers approach their skincare journeys. By leveraging advanced technology, brands like RoC Skincare are empowering individuals to make informed decisions, leading to more effective and satisfying results.

Travel & Adventure

"Life is either a daring adventure or nothing at all." — Helen Keller

Gone are the days of one-size-fits-all travel. Today's journeys are smarter, more intuitive, and tailored to each traveler's unique rhythm—thanks to the quiet genius of AI working behind the scenes. Language is no longer a barrier, solo explorers feel more secure than ever, and every trip becomes a personalized story waiting to unfold. In this section, we explore three powerful case studies that reveal how technology is transforming the way we experience the world.

31. Wanderlust, Powered by AI: How GuideGeek Transforms Travel Dreams into Reality

Planning a vacation can often feel overwhelming, with countless hours spent researching destinations, activities, and accommodations to align with individual preferences. Traditional methods frequently fall short in delivering the personalization needed to cater to unique traveler interests, resulting in generic experiences. The emergence of AI-powered travel assistants has revolutionized this process, offering tailored recommendations that streamline planning and elevate the overall travel experience.

GuideGeek, developed by Matador Network, is an AI-powered travel assistant designed to provide personalized travel recommendations. Accessible through platforms like Instagram, WhatsApp, and Facebook Messenger, GuideGeek utilizes generative AI technology to interact with users in a conversational manner. Travelers can input their preferences—such as desired destinations, activities, budget constraints, and travel dates—and the AI processes this information, cross-referencing it with real-time data from over 1,000 travel-specific integrations, including live flight, hotel, and vacation rental data. It then generates customized itineraries that align with the user's interests and constraints.

For instance, a user seeking a cultural experience in Europe with a moderate budget might receive a detailed plan encompassing visits to historical sites, local culinary experiences, and affordable boutique accommodations. The itineraries are comprehensive, covering daily activities, transportation options, and dining suggestions, all tailored to the user's profile. GuideGeek's ability to engage in multi-turn conversations allows users to iteratively refine their plans, ensuring the final itinerary closely matches their expectations.

A notable real-world example is that of Michael Motamedi and his family, who embarked on a year-long world tour using GuideGeek as their primary travel planner. From exploring traditional markets in Morocco to indulging in culinary adventures in Spain, GuideGeek provided them with accurate local recommendations and unique cultural experiences.

Users of GuideGeek have reported significant improvements in their travel planning experiences. The personalized itineraries save time and reduce the stress associated with organizing trips. Travelers appreciate the AI's ability to uncover hidden gems and provide suggestions that align with their specific interests, leading to more fulfilling and unique travel experiences. The convenience of accessing a comprehensive travel plan through familiar messaging platforms further enhances user satisfaction. Additionally, GuideGeek's integration of real-time data ensures that recommendations are current and relevant, adapting to factors such as weather conditions, local events, and travel advisories.

32. Breaking Language Barriers: Real-Time AI Translation Enhances Global Travel

Language barriers have long posed challenges for international travelers, leading to misunderstandings and limiting cultural immersion. Traditional translation methods, such as phrasebooks or human interpreters, can be cumbersome and not always readily available. The advent of AI-powered real-time translation devices has revolutionized cross-lingual communication, enabling travelers to interact more freely and confidently in foreign environments.

A notable example is the experience of a traveler who visited the Louvre Museum in Paris. Using TravelAI's mobile app, they could point their smartphone camera at exhibit labels or informational panels, and the app instantly overlaid the text with an English translation. This seamless interaction allowed for a deeper understanding and appreciation of the exhibits, fostering a more meaningful connection with the local culture.

Devices like Google's Pixel Buds exemplify the integration of AI in real-time translation. These earbuds offer real-time translation capabilities through Google Translate, allowing users to engage in conversations with speakers of different languages. The device provides instantaneous translations directly into the user's ear, leveraging advanced machine learning algorithms to process and translate speech in real-time, accommodating nuances such as regional accents and colloquialisms. This technology captures spoken language through the device's microphone, transmits the data to cloud-based servers where AI algorithms perform speech recognition and translation, and then delivers the translated speech back to the user. Such seamless interaction fosters more natural conversations without significant delays, enhancing connections between travelers and locals.

Travelers utilizing AI-powered translation devices have reported enhanced communication abilities, leading to more immersive and enjoyable travel experiences. The ability to understand and be understood in real-time opens doors to authentic cultural exchanges, participation in local activities, and access to services that might otherwise be inaccessible due to language constraints. For instance, travelers can confidently navigate public transportation systems, order food in local restaurants, and seek assistance in emergencies. Moreover, businesses in the travel and hospitality industry have adopted similar AI translation technologies to better serve international clients, resulting in improved customer satisfaction and expanded global reach.

33. Wander Wisely: The Rise of AI Guardians for Solo Explorers

Solo travel offers unique opportunities for self-discovery and adventure but also presents specific safety concerns. Travelers venturing alone may face challenges such as navigating unfamiliar areas, staying connected with emergency contacts, and accessing reliable safety information. AI-driven applications have been developed to address these issues, providing solo travelers with tools to enhance their security and confidence while exploring new destinations.

The "Go Solo" app is designed specifically for solo travelers, integrating AI features to ensure user safety and convenience. The app offers functionalities such as real-time location sharing with trusted contacts, AI-curated recommendations for safe accommodations and activities, and instant access to emergency services. Users can input their travel plans, and the AI system analyzes factors like local crime rates, political stability, and health advisories to provide personalized safety tips. Additionally, the app's

AI chatbot can answer travelers' questions about local customs, transportation options, and language assistance, making it a comprehensive companion for solo travelers.

The "Go Solo" app, and others like it such as Noonlight and GeoSure, have been widely adopted by travelers seeking to increase their situational awareness and reduce risks while journeying alone. Users report feeling more confident exploring unfamiliar places, knowing they have tools that proactively monitor their safety and can instantly connect them to help if needed.

One notable feature that has been praised is the "check-in timer" system, which prompts solo travelers to confirm their safety at set intervals. If no response is received, the app automatically notifies emergency contacts and dispatches local assistance through pre-integrated services. In one case, a solo female traveler in South America was able to quickly summon help through the app after her taxi driver unexpectedly altered the route. The AI detected a significant deviation from the expected path and triggered a response before a situation escalated.

Beyond emergency support, the app's AI algorithms help solo travelers make more informed decisions. The risk-rating system, which scores neighborhoods and routes based on real-time crime data and crowd-sourced reports, allows users to reroute their paths or adjust their itineraries to stay within safer areas. Localized insights are especially beneficial in cities where safety conditions vary drastically by neighborhood, empowering users to confidently engage in cultural exploration with less fear of being caught off-guard.

In addition to safety, the app enhances solo travel enjoyment. AI-curated suggestions for well-reviewed solo-friendly cafés, coworking lounges, and local meetups give travelers opportunities to connect with others while maintaining autonomy. In this way, the app supports not only physical safety but also emotional well-being by fostering a sense of connection and agency.

As solo travel continues to rise in popularity, AI-driven platforms like Go Solo are leading the way in making independent exploration safer, smarter, and more fulfilling for everyone—from first-time adventurers to seasoned globetrotters.

Home & Living

"Innovation is not just in how we live, but in how our homes learn to live with us." — Designed for Tomorrow

Imagine a home that not only shelters but also safeguards—where every corner is attuned to your well-being, and unseen guardians work tirelessly to ensure your safety and comfort. Through intelligent systems, our living spaces are evolving into proactive environments that monitor for fire hazards, detect unusual activities, and support the independence of our aging loved ones. In the following section, we delve into three compelling case studies that illustrate how these smart technologies are transforming homes into havens of security and peace of mind.

34. Preventing Fires Before They Spark: How Ting is Revolutionizing Home Safety

Electrical fires pose a significant risk to homeowners, often resulting from undetected faults within a home's electrical system. Traditional smoke detectors alert occupants only after a fire has started, which can be too late to prevent damage or injury. To address this issue, Whisker Labs developed Ting, an AI-powered sensor designed to detect electrical hazards before they escalate into fires.

Ting is a compact device that plugs into any standard electrical outlet. Once installed, it continuously monitors the home's electrical network, analyzing data to identify micro-arcs and other anomalies indicative of potential fire hazards. The device performs approximately 30 million electrical measurements every second, utilizing AI algorithms to detect patterns that may precede electrical fires. When Ting identifies a potential issue, it alerts the homeowner via a smartphone app and provides guidance on mitigating the risk. In some cases, Ting's monitoring service coordinates with licensed electricians to address the problem promptly.

Arthur, a homeowner, experienced firsthand the protective capabilities of Ting. The Ting fire safety team detected an anomalous electrical signal in his home, suggesting a faulty circuit breaker. They guided him through a process of turning off each breaker sequentially while monitoring the signal. Upon identifying the problematic breaker, Arthur ordered a replacement. While awaiting delivery, the faulty breaker began arcing—a serious fire hazard. Thanks to Ting's early detection, Arthur was able to prevent a potential fire by turning off the breaker and installing the new one upon its arrival.

Since its deployment, Ting has been installed in over 700,000 homes across the United States. The device has demonstrated a remarkable ability to prevent electrical fires, with reports indicating that it has detected and mitigated hazards in approximately one out of every 150 homes monitored. This proactive approach has prevented numerous potential fires, safeguarding lives and property. Additionally, the data collected by Ting has provided valuable insights into common electrical issues, contributing to broader efforts in fire prevention and electrical safety.

35. Smart Sentinels: How AI is Revolutionizing Home Security

Traditional home security systems often rely on motion detectors and cameras that can generate numerous false alarms, leading to desensitization and delayed responses. The integration of AI into home security aims to enhance the accuracy and efficiency of threat detection, providing homeowners with more reliable and proactive protection.

Modern AI-powered security systems utilize advanced technologies such as computer vision and machine learning to analyze real-time data from surveillance cameras and sensors. These systems can differentiate between routine activities and potential threats by recognizing patterns and anomalies. For instance, AI algorithms can distinguish between a family member entering the home and an unfamiliar individual loitering near entry points. Some systems also incorporate facial recognition to identify known individuals and alert homeowners to unknown visitors. Additionally, AI enables features like package detection, vehicle recognition, and even the identification of suspicious behaviors, such as someone attempting to tamper with a lock.

A notable example of AI-enhanced security in action is the experience of Laborers Training School, a network of educational campuses in Southern California. Facing challenges in protecting valuable supplies and equipment across multiple locations, the institution partnered with Bay Alarm to implement a customized live video monitoring system. This system utilized AI-enhanced cameras and virtual fence sensors to proactively deter crime. The results were remarkable: zero theft in the first year, $100,000 in prevented losses, and 12+ intrusions thwarted without a single call to the safety manager. The AI-driven approach not only reduced false alarms but also provided real-time alerts, enabling swift responses and enhancing overall security.

The adoption of AI in home security has led to a significant reduction in false alarms and improved response times. Homeowners benefit from more accurate notifications, allowing them to assess situations promptly and take appropriate action. Furthermore, the proactive nature of AI-driven systems means that potential security breaches can be identified and addressed before they escalate. This advancement not only enhances personal safety but also contributes to broader community security efforts by deterring criminal activities.

36. Bridging Generations: How AI Connects Elders and Youth to Fight Isolation

Social isolation and loneliness among older adults living alone are pressing concerns that significantly impact their health and quality of life. Innovative solutions leveraging artificial intelligence (AI) are emerging to address these challenges by providing both practical assistance and social engagement.

Consider the case of *Eldera*, an AI-driven platform founded by Dana Griffin in 2020. Eldera connects adults over 60 with children aged 5 to 18 for weekly video mentoring sessions, fostering intergenerational relationships that combat loneliness and provide a sense of purpose. With nearly 3,000 mentor-mentee pairs and additional children on a waiting list, Eldera exemplifies the positive impact of AI in reducing social isolation among older adults.

AI-powered voice assistants, such as Amazon Alexa™, have also proven effective in mitigating feelings of loneliness among seniors. A study involving older adults using these devices for at least 30 minutes daily over three months revealed significant reductions in loneliness and increased perceived social support. Participants valued the companionship and assistance provided by the voice assistants, integrating them into their daily routines to enhance well-being and independence.

Additional AI Innovations Addressing Loneliness

- ElliQ: An AI-powered robot designed by Intuition Robotics, ElliQ engages seniors in conversation, plays music, provides health reminders, and facilitates communication with family members or emergency services. Users have reported that ElliQ enhances their daily lives through positive interactions and activities.

- CareYaya's QuikTok: This AI phone companion program offers meaningful interactions to older adults, assessing early signs of cognitive decline and supporting mental stimulation and emotional well-being. The program aims to alleviate feelings of loneliness and provide comfort through regular engagement.

Parenting

“Parenting doesn’t come with a manual, but now it comes with an assistant—and that’s been a game-changer for our family.” — Jessica L., early Goldee user and mom of three

Incorporating artificial intelligence (AI) into daily family life has become increasingly prevalent, offering innovative solutions that assist parents in safeguarding their children's online activities, managing daily routines, and addressing the unique needs of children with disabilities. This section delves into three compelling case studies that showcase AI's transformative impact in enhancing online safety, supporting smart parenting, and providing tailored assistance for children with special needs.

37. Digital Guardians: Empowering Parents with AI Tools for Online Safety

In today's digital age, children are exposed to online content more than ever before, with screens being integral to their education, entertainment, and social lives. While the internet offers vast educational opportunities, it also presents significant risks, from cyberbullying to exposure to inappropriate content. For parents, the challenge lies in striking the right balance between allowing children the freedom to explore the digital world and ensuring their safety.

One of the most effective ways to protect children online is through the use of AI-powered tools. These innovative technologies have become essential in providing real-time monitoring, filtering, and protective measures, offering parents peace of mind while navigating the complex digital landscape.

A shining example of this is the development of apps like *Kids Nanny*, an AI-driven solution that has revolutionized the way parents safeguard their children's digital interactions. Once installed on a child's device, Kids Nanny operates quietly in the background, using advanced algorithms to scan screens, analyze online content, and assess digital activity. The app doesn't just passively observe—it actively identifies and flags potentially harmful material, whether it be violent content, adult themes, or predatory behaviors.

For instance, if a child stumbles upon inappropriate content on a social media platform or in an online game, Kids Nanny's AI algorithms will instantly alert parents, offering a detailed report of what the child accessed and where. This real-time information allows parents to step in quickly and address any concerns before they escalate.

Moreover, the app goes beyond simple content filtering by actively monitoring text messages, social media activity, and even email exchanges. This comprehensive approach helps detect subtle signs of cyberbullying, online harassment, or dangerous behaviors—warning parents of potential issues before they become crises. The app's ability to detect patterns over time also helps parents identify any shifts in their child's behavior or online interactions that might indicate deeper issues, such as mental health struggles or negative peer influences.

A powerful real-life example of AI tools transforming parenting is the story of Dr. Lee, a mother of two and a child psychologist who saw firsthand the dangers of the digital world. After her daughter faced online harassment, Dr. Lee implemented AI tools to monitor her children's online interactions. Over time, she noticed a significant reduction in online threats, as the AI software was able to identify subtle signs of cyberbullying before they escalated. Dr. Lee has since become an advocate for AI-powered parental controls, speaking at conferences about how technology can empower parents to create a safer, more supportive environment for their children in an increasingly digital world.

In addition to enhancing safety, AI tools like Kids Nanny help foster meaningful conversations between parents and children about digital responsibility. With insights drawn from the app's reports, parents are equipped to discuss issues like privacy, respectful communication, and online etiquette, helping children grow into responsible digital citizens. These discussions, guided by data, create a foundation for healthy, open conversations about the challenges and opportunities of the digital age.

The integration of AI into parental monitoring has brought a transformative shift in online child safety. By enabling real-time alerts, comprehensive activity tracking, and proactive intervention, these tools give parents the knowledge they need to keep their children safe while navigating the online world. With AI as an ally, parents can now face the challenges of the digital age with confidence, ensuring their children's well-being while fostering an environment of trust and communication.

Additional AI Tools for Parental Control

- Bark: This application scans text messages, social media platforms, web browsers, and emails to alert parents about potential risks, including cyberbullying and inappropriate content.

- Qustodio: Offering comprehensive monitoring, Qustodio enables parents to oversee device usage, set screen time limits, and filter content, ensuring a balanced digital environment for their children.
- Aura: Aura's AI-powered app provides parents with insights into their children's online activities, tracking sleep patterns, monitoring social interactions, and detecting significant emotional shifts to facilitate balanced conversations about their digital lives.

38. From Chaos to Calm: How AI Tools are Helping Families Find Balance

Parenting in the modern world often feels like juggling a million responsibilities—managing work, ensuring children's education, overseeing extracurricular activities, and maintaining a household. For many parents, the weight of these duties can be overwhelming, leading to stress and burnout. But in the age of technology, a new breed of smart assistants is stepping in to help. AI-powered tools are offering much-needed support, not just in managing schedules, but in fostering healthier family dynamics and promoting a balanced, organized home environment.

One such innovation is the Skylight Calendar Max, a sleek, 27-inch touchscreen hub that's more than just a family calendar—it's a central organizational tool designed to streamline household tasks. This device synchronizes the calendars of every family member, displaying daily schedules, chore charts, to-do lists, and even meal plans. With everything in one place, the Skylight Calendar Max makes it easier than ever for parents to stay on top of their family's needs and commitments.

What truly sets Skylight Calendar Max apart is its integration with the accompanying app, *Sidekick*. This AI-powered assistant takes the stress out of meal planning and grocery shopping by generating customized meal plans based on each family member's preferences, dietary restrictions, and even seasonal ingredients. It then creates grocery lists to match, streamlining the shopping process and ensuring that healthy, well-balanced meals are always on the table.

Parents who have adopted Skylight Calendar Max report significant improvements in their daily routines. Not only has it reduced the time spent coordinating schedules, but it has also helped alleviate the mental load that often falls solely on the parents. With automated tasks like meal planning and household organization, families are experiencing more free time and reduced stress levels, allowing for greater focus on spending quality time together.

What's more, the app isn't just for the adults. The intuitive interface of the Skylight Calendar Max allows even young children to interact with it. Whether it's checking off their chores, adding events to the calendar, or simply understanding the family's daily flow, children are learning valuable lessons in responsibility, organization, and teamwork. The inclusion of all family members in managing the household promotes a sense of unity and shared purpose, reinforcing the idea that everyone plays a part in keeping the home running smoothly.

A real-world example of how this AI-powered tool has changed the dynamic in a family is the story of Sarah, a mother of three who found herself overwhelmed by the competing demands of work, school activities, and daily household tasks. "Before we had the Skylight Calendar Max, I was constantly scrambling to keep everything organized," Sarah recalls. "But now, everything is in one place, and my kids can help too. They love the chore chart feature, and it has made them more responsible."

In fact, Sarah noticed a shift in the family dynamic. Her children were not just following schedules—they were taking ownership of tasks, with the older ones helping their younger siblings understand what needed to be done. Her own stress levels dropped dramatically, and she found more time to relax with her family instead of running around managing logistics.

The effect on family communication has been equally profound. Instead of endless back-and-forth about who's doing what, the Skylight Calendar Max facilitates more transparent communication. With everyone on the same page, there's less confusion and fewer conflicts, allowing the family to focus on the things that truly matter—connection, quality time, and shared experiences.

The integration of AI into family management isn't just about convenience; it's about transforming how families function together. By taking care of mundane tasks, these tools are giving parents the gift of time and mental clarity, allowing them to focus on the deeper, more meaningful aspects of family life. With the support of AI, families are not only staying organized—they're thriving.

39. Bridging the Gap: AI's Role in Enhancing Social Skills for Children with Special Needs

Children with special needs often face challenges that go beyond traditional learning obstacles, requiring a deeply personalized approach to their education and development. While every child's needs are unique, there is one thing all children, including those with Autism Spectrum Disorder (ASD), share in common: the desire to connect, learn, and grow. However, for children with ASD, social interactions, emotional understanding, and communication can be particularly difficult. This is where the power of technology, specifically AI, has the potential to make a profound difference.

One of the most groundbreaking advancements in this field is the Autism Glass Project by Stanford University. This innovative project uses wearable technology—specifically Google Glass—combined with AI and machine learning to offer real-time support for children with ASD. The device is equipped with sophisticated algorithms that can recognize and interpret facial expressions, a fundamental aspect of social communication that can often be a challenge for children with autism.

The system works by analyzing the faces of people around the child, interpreting emotional cues such as happiness, sadness, anger, and surprise. The device then provides immediate, personalized feedback to the child through auditory or visual signals, helping them recognize and understand the emotions of others. This is a crucial tool for children who may struggle with social cues, as it gives them a clearer understanding of how others are feeling and how to appropriately respond.

One of the most inspiring examples of this technology in action comes from a young boy named Ethan, a 9-year-old with ASD who was struggling with social interactions and emotional recognition. His parents, after hearing about the Autism Glass Project, decided to enroll him in a clinical trial. Before using the glasses, Ethan found it difficult to understand the emotions of his peers, which led to social isolation and frustration.

After just a few weeks of using the glasses, Ethan's parents saw a noticeable improvement. He began to better interpret emotions like happiness and sadness, and his interactions with other children became more engaged. For instance, when he saw a classmate smiling, the glasses would alert him, and he learned to smile back, recognizing that it was a positive social cue. The feedback helped Ethan gain the confidence to engage in conversations and make new friends.

Clinical evaluations of the Autism Glass system have confirmed these improvements. Children who used the device showed greater social engagement and better communication skills, enhancing their ability to navigate both school and social settings. Educators and parents reported increased participation in group activities, more eye contact, and a greater understanding of social norms.

The success of the Autism Glass Project demonstrates the incredible potential of AI to support children with special needs, providing them with the tools to navigate the world in ways that were previously unimaginable. By bridging the gap between the child's experience and the social world around them, AI is not just improving learning outcomes; it is fostering inclusion, empathy, and understanding.

For parents and educators, these advancements offer a new sense of hope. AI technology is not a substitute for human connection but a powerful tool that can enhance how children with special needs experience the world. As more children gain access to such tools, we can expect to see more confident, engaged, and socially integrated individuals—equipped with the skills and support they need to thrive.

In the case of Ethan and so many other children, AI is not just a tool; it's a bridge that connects them to the world in ways that empower them to be themselves and build meaningful relationships. The Autism Glass Project is a shining example of how technology can support children in their educational and emotional development, creating a more inclusive world where every child has the opportunity to flourish.

Love & Relationships

"The best thing to hold onto in life is each other." — Audrey Hepburn

In today's world, technology is reshaping how we connect and nurture our most important relationships. From finding a soulmate to maintaining strong bonds across distances, innovations are transforming the way couples meet, communicate, and resolve conflicts. This section highlights three inspiring stories that demonstrate how cutting-edge tools are enhancing romantic relationships, fostering deeper connections, and helping couples navigate the complexities of love in the modern age.

40. Beyond the Swipe: How the Aphrodite Project is Shaping Lasting Relationships with AI

In a world where modern relationships often begin with a simple swipe or a click, the quest for love can feel overwhelming and, at times, disconnected. While online dating platforms have offered convenience, they have also highlighted the challenge of truly understanding compatibility in the digital realm. But now, with the advent of artificial intelligence, the landscape of matchmaking is evolving into something far more sophisticated, meaningful, and personal.

One of the most inspiring examples of this transformation is the Aphrodite Project, an annual matchmaking event designed to revolutionize how university students find meaningful connections. Launched in 2019, the project integrates machine learning algorithms to match individuals based on comprehensive questionnaires that assess not only basic preferences but also deeper factors such as personality traits, values, and lifestyle choices. This thoughtful approach goes beyond surface-level interests, delving into the emotional and intellectual compatibility of participants.

The success of the Aphrodite Project is undeniable. Since its inception, over 85,000 individuals have participated, leading to over 6 marriages and countless long-term relationships. The AI system behind the project analyzes vast amounts of data, processing responses to the questionnaires and identifying patterns that lead to meaningful matches. By focusing on a holistic view of compatibility, participants are paired with individuals who share their core values and life goals, offering a far more tailored and lasting connection than many traditional methods of matchmaking.

The impact on participants is profound. Unlike the often random nature of swiping or superficial online connections, the AI-powered matching process leads to deeper, more satisfying relationships. Take the story of Emily and Daniel, two university students who met through the Aphrodite Project. Both had spent years on dating apps with limited success, often feeling frustrated by the mismatch between their values and the people they were meeting. But when they were matched through the project, they found something different—genuine connection. "It felt like the system really understood who we were," Emily says. "It wasn't just about shared interests; it was about shared values and what we wanted out of life." Emily and Daniel have now been together for two years and credit their successful relationship to the thoughtful, data-driven process of the Aphrodite Project.

For many, the satisfaction with the matches goes beyond the event itself. Participants have reported a deeper sense of fulfillment in their relationships, as the AI system facilitates connections that feel natural and authentic. Rather than relying on chance or superficial traits, the AI-backed approach focuses on long-term compatibility, which leads to stronger, more enduring partnerships.

The story of the Aphrodite Project illustrates a powerful evolution in the world of matchmaking. By using AI to analyze human connection on a deeper level, it's creating more meaningful relationships that are built on shared values and long-term potential. As AI continues to refine its ability to understand human dynamics, the future of dating looks brighter than ever—where finding love is not just a matter of luck, but of intelligent, insightful matching that leads to truly life-changing connections.

41. Love Across Miles: How VR is Revolutionizing Intimacy in Long-Distance Relationships

Long-distance relationships are a test of both emotional strength and creativity. While love knows no physical boundaries, the distance between partners often creates a sense of longing and isolation, challenging couples to find new ways to stay emotionally connected. In recent years, technological innovations, especially in the realms of virtual reality (VR) and artificial intelligence (AI), have provided fresh solutions to bridge the emotional gap between lovers separated by miles.

One groundbreaking development is a virtual reality (VR) application designed specifically to foster intimacy in long-distance relationships. This VR app incorporates a unique twist: it combines the power of Loving-Kindness Meditation (LKM) with immersive technology, allowing partners to engage in shared meditation experiences that deepen emotional connection and promote mindfulness. The app is designed to create a virtual space where couples can sit together—despite the physical distance—and meditate, practice compassion, and foster a sense of love and togetherness.

The development of this VR LKM app wasn't just a technical endeavor—it involved heartfelt workshops with real couples to ensure the technology met their emotional needs. The developers sought feedback from participants about their experiences and desires in maintaining closeness, which allowed the app to evolve into a tool that's not just functional, but deeply meaningful.

The results have been incredibly positive. Couples who have used the VR LKM application report a marked increase in their emotional connection. For instance, Sarah and Tom, a couple who have been living in different countries for several years, found that the VR app gave them a powerful way to stay close. "We've tried all sorts of ways to maintain intimacy, but nothing felt as real as when we could meditate together, even though we were so far apart," Sarah says. "It was like we could share a peaceful moment without distractions, just us in the moment, together."

The app's immersive nature fosters a sense of shared presence, where each partner can visualize their loved one in the virtual space, engaging in deep meditation and cultivating loving-kindness toward one another. This not only reduces feelings of loneliness and isolation but also promotes a sense of mindfulness, helping partners remain grounded in love and gratitude. For couples like Sarah and Tom, this has transformed their relationship, reducing stress and creating an emotional bond that feels stronger than ever, despite the miles that separate them.

In addition to meditation, the app allows for personalized experiences, enabling couples to customize the environment, sounds, and even the type of meditation practice they engage in. This flexibility allows for the deepening of intimacy over time, as partners can explore different practices together and create shared rituals that transcend physical space.

What's truly remarkable about the VR LKM application is how it highlights the power of technology to enhance emotional well-being. It's not just about bridging physical distances; it's about strengthening the emotional and psychological connection between partners. With the help of AI and VR, couples can now experience moments of profound intimacy, shared presence, and mindfulness, offering a glimpse into a future where technology can serve as an ally in fostering love, even across great distances.

The success of this project has opened the door for future innovations in relationship support. As AI and VR technologies continue to evolve, we may soon see even more advanced tools that allow couples to stay emotionally connected, no matter the physical challenges they face. In a world that's becoming more interconnected digitally, the possibility of maintaining deep, loving relationships, regardless of location, has never seemed more achievable.

42. AI Assists in Relationship Communication and Conflict Resolution

Effective communication is often the foundation upon which strong, lasting relationships are built. Yet, in the heat of disagreement, it's easy for emotions to overwhelm even the most loving couples. Navigating conflict can be tricky, and finding a way to communicate that fosters understanding rather than division requires patience and skill. Enter AI-powered tools, which are increasingly being used to assist couples in improving their communication and resolving conflicts in a calm and productive manner.

One of the most innovative tools in this space is the use of AI chatbots, like ChatGPT, as relationship mediators. These AI systems are not just programmed to respond to queries—they are designed to analyze the context of disputes and offer impartial advice, helping partners navigate the tricky terrain of conflict resolution. When couples find themselves in the midst of a disagreement, they can input the details into an AI chatbot, which then analyzes the situation and provides thoughtful suggestions for resolving the conflict. Whether it's offering advice on how to express feelings without causing harm or suggesting a more empathetic way to listen, the AI helps de-escalate tension and foster more productive, respectful conversations.

This technology is already proving to be a valuable asset for many couples. Take Rachel and Javier, for example. After five years of living together, they found themselves caught in repetitive cycles of misunderstanding. Simple disagreements would escalate into major arguments, and they struggled to find common ground. "We just weren't hearing each other," Rachel admits. "We would both get defensive, and the conversation would spiral."

When a friend recommended using an AI chatbot to mediate their arguments, Rachel and Javier were initially skeptical. But after trying it, they found the experience unexpectedly helpful. By entering the details of their conflict into the chatbot, they received a neutral, third-party perspective that helped them see the issue from a different angle. "The chatbot didn't take sides," Javier explains. "It gave us both space to express ourselves and helped us focus on finding a solution rather than blaming each other." Over time, they began to notice that their communication improved, and conflicts no longer escalated into major issues. The AI-mediated sessions encouraged them to slow down and approach each other with more patience and empathy.

Couples using AI chatbots have reported that these tools help prevent arguments from escalating by fostering a more open and understanding environment. The neutrality of the AI—free from bias or emotional attachment—allows for more honest discussions. It also provides a space for partners to reflect on their feelings before they respond, which can lead to healthier communication patterns overall.

While AI-powered communication tools are certainly making waves in relationship support, experts remind couples that these tools are most effective when used for everyday communication issues. For more complex or deeply rooted relationship challenges, professional counseling and therapy remain essential. AI tools can't replace the nuanced understanding and expertise that a trained counselor provides. However, when used to address minor conflicts or to reinforce healthier communication habits, these tools offer a powerful, accessible resource for couples who want to build stronger relationships.

The future of relationships may well involve a harmonious blend of human connection and technological assistance. As AI continues to evolve, it will only become better at helping couples navigate the challenges of modern relationships, fostering deeper understanding, empathy, and emotional intimacy.

Personal Productivity

"You may delay, but time will not." — Benjamin Franklin

Boosting personal productivity and fostering meaningful growth has never been more achievable, thanks to intelligent tools that automate tasks, reduce distractions, and encourage self-reflection. From dynamic to-do lists that adapt to your priorities, to focus-enhancing apps that protect your time, and even smart journaling platforms that guide introspection, these technologies are helping individuals reclaim their time and energy. This section highlights three inspiring case studies where such tools have empowered people to streamline their lives, stay present, and unlock new levels of efficiency and personal development.

43. From Overwhelmed to In Control: The Smart Way to Master Your Tasks

Staying on top of daily responsibilities can feel like an endless juggling act—especially when priorities shift, deadlines loom, and motivation wanes. Traditional to-do lists, while useful, often lack the flexibility and insight needed to truly keep up with modern life. Enter the next generation of productivity tools: AI-powered task managers that don't just remind you of what to do, but *when* and *how* to do it most effectively.

One standout example of this transformation is Todoist, a popular task management app that now includes a game-changing feature called Smart Schedule. This AI-driven system analyzes your past behavior, current workload, and upcoming deadlines to intelligently suggest the best times to complete each task. Rather than relying on guesswork or rigid schedules, users are guided by real-time insights that adapt to their personal rhythms and priorities.

Take the story of David, a product designer and father of two, who found himself constantly overwhelmed by an ever-growing to-do list. "I'd plan my day every morning, but by noon everything was off track," he recalls. "I wasn't just falling behind—I was burning out." When he started using Todoist's Smart Schedule, things began to shift. The AI not only helped him reorder tasks based on urgency and available time, but also encouraged healthier pacing by spacing out intense work with lighter activities. "It felt like I had a personal productivity coach," David says. "I wasn't just ticking boxes—I was actually getting the right things done at the right time."

The results? David reclaimed hours in his week, felt more in control, and experienced less stress. "It gave me back the headspace to be present with my kids after work. That's priceless."

Stories like David's illustrate how AI-enhanced to-do lists are more than digital planners—they're intelligent partners in your daily life. By offloading the mental strain of decision-making and time-blocking, these tools empower users to focus on execution, creativity, and balance. With productivity personalized to your lifestyle, the path to getting things done becomes smoother—and far more sustainable.

44. Freedom to Flourish: Unlocking Deep Work in a Distracted World

In a world buzzing with pings, notifications, and endless tabs, protecting our attention has become a modern-day superpower. The ability to focus deeply—not just for minutes, but for meaningful stretches of time—is increasingly rare and incredibly valuable. That's why a new wave of AI-powered focus tools is transforming the way people work, helping them reclaim their concentration and unlock peak productivity.

One standout example is Freedom, a cross-device app that doesn't just block distracting websites and apps—it *learns* your habits. With the help of AI, Freedom analyzes usage patterns to identify when your focus is at risk and recommends optimal work times. It even anticipates potential distractions before they derail your day, enabling you to enter a flow state more effortlessly and stay there longer.

Consider the story of Katherine, a freelance writer and mom of three who struggled to carve out uninterrupted writing time between client deadlines and household chaos. "I love what I do, but I was constantly fighting the urge to check email or scroll social media," she says. "By the time I found focus, half my work window was gone." That changed when she started using Freedom. The app began learning her natural productivity peaks—late morning and early evening—and suggested focused writing blocks at those times. It also gently nudged her to log off distracting apps during low-focus periods. "The first week I used it, I finished a project two days early," Katherine beams. "Now, I actually *look forward* to my focus sessions."

Katherine's story is one of many that highlight the deeper impact of AI focus tools. It's not just about getting more done—it's about experiencing the satisfaction that comes from *immersing* yourself in your craft, uninterrupted. These tools offer users a path back to mental clarity, helping them produce higher-quality work, feel more in control of their time, and walk away from their desks with a genuine sense of accomplishment.

In an age where attention is a commodity, tools like Freedom are quietly leading a digital renaissance—one where silence, stillness, and focus make space for brilliance.

45. Pages of Progress: How AI Journaling is Rewriting the Story of Self-Discovery

Journaling has long been a gateway to self-discovery, emotional healing, and personal growth. Yet in the whirlwind of daily life, many people struggle to maintain the habit, unsure of what to write or how to start. Now, a new generation of AI-assisted journaling tools is reigniting this timeless practice—making self-reflection more accessible, personalized, and powerful than ever before.

Enter MindScape, an innovative journaling app that merges behavioral data with the capabilities of Large Language Models (LLMs) to deliver a transformative writing experience. Unlike traditional journaling apps that offer generic prompts, MindScape tailors its suggestions based on your unique daily rhythms—analyzing data like sleep quality, social engagement, and emotional tone. The result? Thoughtful, deeply relevant prompts that meet you exactly where you are, whether you're celebrating a win or navigating a difficult day.

A powerful example comes from Alicia, a high school teacher and mother of one, who turned to MindScape after feeling burnt out and emotionally drained. "I've always wanted to journal more, but by the end of the day, I never knew where to begin," Alicia shares. "MindScape's prompts felt like someone truly understood what I was going through." On a day when Alicia had a difficult conversation with a student, the app prompted her with: *"What do you need to let go of to make space for compassion?"*—a question that led to an emotional breakthrough. "It helped me process things I didn't even realize I was holding on to," she says.

Since using the app, Alicia reports improved mental clarity, a deeper connection with her emotions, and a renewed sense of balance. "It's become a ritual I actually look forward to—it feels like therapy in my pocket," she says.

Stories like Alicia's reveal the profound impact of AI-assisted journaling: it doesn't just help people *write*—it helps them *feel*, *heal*, and *grow*. By guiding users through meaningful reflection with empathetic intelligence, apps like MindScape are creating safe, private spaces for emotional growth and self-discovery. In a world that often pulls us outward, these tools gently guide us inward—where the real transformation begins.

Career Transformation

"Choose a job you love, and you will never have to work a day in your life." — Confucius

The modern career landscape is undergoing a remarkable transformation, driven by cutting-edge tools that empower individuals to reskill, adapt, and grow like never before. From personalized learning paths to intelligent career coaching, these innovations are opening doors for people to reinvent themselves professionally, whether they're navigating industry shifts or pursuing entirely new passions. This section highlights three inspiring case studies that showcase how technology is reshaping career development and making lifelong learning a dynamic, personalized journey.

46. From Highway to High-Tech: How One Man Reinvented Himself in the Age of AI

As the world races forward with AI innovations, the job market is evolving just as rapidly—reshaping traditional roles and giving rise to entirely new ones. One of the most exciting of these is prompt engineering, a field where creativity, language, and logic intersect to guide AI systems toward accurate, meaningful outputs. What's truly remarkable is that this emerging profession is welcoming individuals from all walks of life, including those whose jobs have been displaced by automation.

Take the inspiring story of Alex Ramirez, a former long-haul truck driver whose livelihood was upended by the growing presence of autonomous vehicles. Facing an uncertain future, Alex didn't just seek another job—he sought a transformation. With curiosity and grit, he enrolled in an AI reskilling program tailored to prepare everyday professionals for the world of prompt engineering. The program, designed for accessibility and impact, covered everything from the basics of AI and natural language processing to the art of crafting precise, effective prompts. Through immersive projects, real-world simulations, and one-on-one mentorship, Alex not only learned to speak the language of AI but began to shape it.

Upon graduation, Alex landed a role as a prompt engineer at a forward-thinking tech company specializing in generative AI tools. He now collaborates with developers, researchers, and content teams to fine-tune AI interactions, ensuring systems deliver value, clarity, and creativity to users across the globe. "I never thought I'd go from the driver's seat of a truck to steering conversations with AI," Alex shares. "It's not just a new job—it's a new purpose."

Alex's story is a powerful testament to how targeted reskilling initiatives can unlock potential, transform lives, and turn disruption into opportunity. In this age of rapid change, careers are no longer defined by where you start, but by how boldly you're willing to adapt and grow. With the right support, anyone—regardless of background—can pivot into a future-ready role and thrive in the digital economy.

47. From Layoff to Liftoff: How AI Reskilling Sparked a New Career Chapter

As industries evolve under the influence of automation and AI, many workers find themselves at a crossroads—facing job loss, yet standing on the edge of new opportunity. What was once viewed as the end of a career can now become the beginning of a powerful transformation. At the heart of this shift are AI-powered reskilling platforms like SkyHive, which are revolutionizing how individuals transition into meaningful, future-ready roles.

SkyHive, a cloud-based workforce intelligence platform, doesn't just offer generic advice or broad upskilling paths—it maps each person's unique skill set, identifies gaps, and recommends personalized learning journeys aligned with real-time labor market demands. This precision approach makes reskilling faster, more effective, and far more empowering.

One inspiring example is Tina, a former textile factory supervisor in Vancouver who was laid off after 18 years when her company shut down amid global shifts in manufacturing. With limited tech experience and a family to support, Tina turned to SkyHive for direction. The platform assessed her existing strengths—such as team coordination, logistics, and process optimization—and aligned her with training in healthcare operations, a field desperate for talent with those exact skills. Within six months, Tina earned her certification as a medical office administrator and secured a role at a local health clinic. "I thought I'd aged out of opportunity," she says, "but I discovered I still had so much to offer—just in a new way."

Tina's journey is just one of many, demonstrating how AI doesn't have to be a threat to workers—it can be their strongest ally. By connecting potential with purpose, SkyHive and platforms like it are helping to build a more adaptable, inclusive, and empowered workforce, where no one is left behind in the digital revolution.

48. Coached by Code: How AI Mentors Are Unlocking Human Potential

In today's ever-changing job market, finding the right career path can feel like navigating a maze without a map. Many individuals—especially those switching industries, re-entering the workforce, or unsure of their direction—face confusion, self-doubt, and lack of access to meaningful guidance. That's where AI-powered career coaches like Celeste, developed by *BuildWithin*, are changing lives.

Celeste isn't just a chatbot—it's a deeply intuitive digital mentor that engages users in reflective conversations to uncover their *hidden strengths*, passions, and goals. Using this insight, it identifies transferable skills, recommends in-demand career paths, and provides personalized learning plans to help users bridge any gaps. It also connects individuals to training programs and job opportunities aligned with their interests and current labor market needs.

One inspiring success story is Jorge, a 42-year-old hospitality worker from Austin, Texas, who was laid off during the pandemic. With a young daughter to support and few job prospects in his previous field, Jorge turned to Celeste after hearing about it through a local workforce development program. Through a series of personalized assessments and conversations, Celeste helped Jorge recognize his strengths in customer service, team management, and logistics. The platform recommended a transition into *project coordination*—a role he had never considered. It guided him through a targeted online training program and connected him with job openings at local tech firms. Within five months, Jorge landed a position at a software company, earning a higher salary than he had in hospitality, with remote flexibility and room to grow.

"Celeste didn't just help me find a new job," Jorge reflects. "It helped me *see myself differently*. It gave me the confidence and tools to build a new future."

Stories like Jorge's are becoming more common as AI democratizes access to career coaching, helping people from all walks of life step into roles that match their abilities and aspirations. By personalizing guidance at scale, platforms like Celeste are not just reshaping careers—they're reshaping lives.

Real Estate & Property

"Ninety percent of all millionaires become so through owning real estate." — Andrew Carnegie

The real estate and property sector is undergoing a powerful transformation, driven by tools that enhance predictive insights, streamline client interactions, and optimize rental pricing with remarkable precision. From personalized buyer experiences to dynamic pricing strategies and smarter property recommendations, these innovations are reshaping how professionals and clients navigate the housing market. This section highlights three compelling case studies that illustrate the real-world impact of these technologies in action.

49. Tomorrow's Hotspot, Today: How AI is Redrawing the Real Estate Map

Spotting the "next big neighborhood" before it takes off is the holy grail for real estate investors—but intuition and historical trends can only go so far. Now, data-driven foresight is rewriting the rules of property investment. By leveraging machine learning models, researchers and investors can decode the hidden signals of neighborhood evolution—long before cranes dot the skyline or property prices surge.

A standout example comes from the Urban Institute, where researchers built a machine learning system capable of predicting neighborhood development with surprising accuracy. The model analyzes diverse and dynamic datasets, including home values, income levels, education statistics, employment rates, and even subtle demographic shifts. What once took years of on-the-ground research and guesswork can now be identified with a few algorithmic sweeps—offering a time machine into urban transformation.

Take the real-life success story of Nikki, a Detroit-based investor who had long been passionate about equitable urban renewal. After learning about AI-driven forecasting, she adopted a tool based on the Urban Institute's approach. With it, she pinpointed a neighborhood just outside Detroit's downtown core that showed quiet but promising signals—small upticks in local business activity, steady population growth, and improvements in school ratings. Trusting the data, Nikki acquired several properties before prices jumped. Within two years, the neighborhood saw a 30% increase in average home values, and her decision positioned her not only for financial success but also as a community builder. She now partners with nonprofits to ensure affordability remains part of the neighborhood's story.

This fusion of technology and social insight demonstrates how AI isn't just transforming real estate returns—it's empowering smarter, more inclusive development. By helping investors anticipate growth responsibly, AI is shaping a future where opportunity can be both profitable and principled.

50. AI Chatbots Enhance Lead Conversion for Realtors

In today's fast-paced real estate market, staying ahead of the competition requires more than just great listings and expert knowledge—it demands quick, efficient, and personalized communication. With potential clients expecting immediate responses, real estate agents are turning to AI-powered chatbots to ensure no opportunity slips through the cracks. These intelligent systems can handle everything from answering initial inquiries to qualifying leads, all while giving agents more time to focus on what they do best: closing deals.

One standout example is Sterling Property Consultants, a prominent real estate agency that integrated an AI chatbot developed by Yogreet into their customer engagement strategy. The chatbot was designed to seamlessly interact with potential clients, answering property questions, providing detailed information, and even scheduling viewings—all in real-time. By automating these interactions, Sterling Estates was able to ensure clients received prompt responses, creating an experience that felt both personalized and immediate. Clients could easily access property details and book appointments without the frustration of waiting for an agent's availability.

The results were striking. Sterling Property Consultants reported a dramatic increase in both lead management efficiency and conversion rates. With the chatbot handling routine queries and appointment scheduling, the sales team could dedicate their energy to nurturing high-value leads and closing more deals.

By adopting this technology, Sterling Property Consultants not only enhanced client satisfaction but also achieved a more streamlined and profitable workflow. The success of their AI-driven customer service model is a testament to the power of integrating cutting-edge technology with human expertise, creating a winning formula for both agents and clients alike.

51. Smart Pricing for Smarter Profits: How AI is Transforming Real Estate Rentals

Setting the right rental price is crucial for property managers striving to balance profitability with tenant retention. Traditionally, this has involved a blend of market knowledge and intuition, but the advent of AI-driven analytics has introduced a more precise and data-backed approach to determining the optimal price point. By analyzing a variety of factors, such as local economic trends, competitor pricing, and property-specific conditions, AI platforms are helping property managers make more informed, strategic decisions.

One inspiring example of this innovative approach is the collaboration between Beekin, an AI solutions provider, and a leading build-to-rent real estate developer. Together, they launched LeaseMax, an AI-powered platform specifically designed to optimize rental pricing. The platform taps into vast datasets, processing market trends, occupancy rates, and economic indicators to suggest the most competitive pricing strategies for each individual unit. LeaseMax's ability to continuously adapt to real-time market shifts means that rental prices can be dynamically adjusted, ensuring units are priced accurately in relation to demand, neighborhood trends, and seasonal fluctuations.

The results have been remarkable. By deploying LeaseMax, the developer saw a significant $300,000 increase in profits, thanks to a more efficient lease-up process and better-aligned rental prices. "LeaseMax allowed us to quickly adjust our prices based on real-time market data, which helped us fill units faster and at higher rates than before," said a project manager involved in the implementation. This approach not only accelerated leasing but also improved revenue management, enabling the developer to maintain competitive pricing throughout fluctuating market conditions.

What's especially inspiring about this story is how AI technology is transforming traditionally complex industries like real estate, providing accessible tools for growth and profitability. With AI platforms like LeaseMax, property managers and developers are better equipped to navigate the often unpredictable rental market and maximize returns while maintaining tenant satisfaction.

E-Commerce and Retail

"Your most unhappy customers are your greatest source of learning." — Bill Gates

Personalized experiences, dynamic pricing, and intelligent inventory management are redefining the future of e-commerce and retail. By harnessing data-driven insights and automation, businesses are not only anticipating customer needs with greater accuracy but also streamlining operations and boosting profitability. This section highlights three powerful case studies that showcase the transformative potential of these innovations in action.

52. Styling the Future: How AI Personalization Transformed Online Fashion Retail

In the fiercely competitive world of online fashion retail, delivering a personalized shopping experience has become essential for engaging customers and driving sales. Recognizing this, a leading online fashion retailer partnered with Zignuts Technolab to implement an AI-powered recommendation engine tailored to their diverse customer base. This advanced system analyzed user behavior, purchase history, and real-time browsing data to generate personalized product suggestions. By continuously refining its recommendations through machine learning algorithms, the engine ensured that customers received relevant and accurate product options, enhancing their shopping experience and encouraging exploration of a wider product range.

The impact of this AI integration was significant. Within the first quarter post-implementation, the retailer experienced a 20% increase in sales, a 15% rise in time spent on the site, and a 25% boost in conversion rates. These improvements not only elevated the shopping experience but also fostered greater customer satisfaction and loyalty, contributing to sustained revenue growth.

For instance, consider Maya, a frequent online shopper who often felt overwhelmed by the vast array of options. After the implementation of the AI recommendation engine, Maya found that the product suggestions aligned closely with her style preferences and past purchases. This personalized approach made her shopping experience more enjoyable and efficient, leading her to make more purchases and become a loyal customer.

53. The Future of Pricing: AI-Driven Strategies Boosting Retail Profitability

Dynamic pricing is a critical strategy in retail, allowing businesses to adjust prices based on market demand, competition, and other external factors. AI-powered pricing engines have revolutionized this approach by enabling real-time price optimization to maximize revenue and profitability.

A prominent online marketplace aimed to enhance its pricing strategy to remain competitive and boost revenue. The company collaborated with Clarion Technologies to develop and implement an AI-driven dynamic pricing engine. This system utilized sophisticated algorithms to analyze vast datasets, including competitor pricing, market trends, and customer behavior. By processing this information in real-time, the engine could adjust product prices dynamically, ensuring optimal pricing that balanced competitiveness with profitability. The AI system's continuous learning capabilities allowed it to adapt to changing market conditions and refine pricing strategies accordingly.

The deployment of the AI-powered pricing engine resulted in a 12% increase in revenue for the online marketplace. Additionally, the company experienced a 15% improvement in market share, reflecting its enhanced competitive positioning. Profit margins also saw an 8% uplift, demonstrating the effectiveness of the dynamic pricing strategy in optimizing financial performance. These outcomes underscored the value of integrating AI into pricing strategies to respond agilely to market dynamics and consumer demand.

54. Retailers Use AI to Automate Inventory Management

In the dynamic world of retail, efficient inventory management is vital to meet customer demand while minimizing costs. One of the world's largest retailers, has embraced AI-driven solutions to revolutionize its inventory processes. By analyzing real-time data on sales, traffic patterns, fuel costs, and weather conditions, their AI systems provide insights into demand patterns and logistical considerations. This enables informed decisions about stock levels and distribution, ensuring products are available when and where customers need them. The integration of AI has led to more accurate demand forecasting and efficient stock replenishment, reducing instances of overstocking and stockouts. Additionally, the AI-driven approach has enhanced supply chain efficiency by optimizing delivery routes and reducing logistical costs, exemplifying how technology can drive operational excellence in retail.

Consider the experience of Emily, a store manager at a one of world's largest big box retailers in Dallas. Before the AI implementation, Emily often grappled with stock discrepancies, leading to customer dissatisfaction. With the new AI system, she receives predictive insights that help maintain optimal inventory levels. "The AI tools have transformed our inventory management. We can now anticipate demand more accurately and ensure our shelves are stocked appropriately," Emily noted. This technological advancement not only streamlined operations but also enhanced the shopping experience for customers.

Environment & Climate

"A great city is not to be confounded with a populous one." — Aristotle

Tackling some of the planet's most pressing environmental challenges, cutting-edge technologies are helping predict wildfires, monitor deforestation, and optimize energy consumption in cities. Through powerful data analysis and real-time insights, these innovations are enabling faster, smarter responses that protect ecosystems, reduce carbon footprints, and promote sustainable urban living. This section explores three compelling case studies that showcase how intelligent systems are transforming environmental stewardship.

55. Predicting the Flames: How AI is Revolutionizing Wildfire Management

In an era where wildfires are intensifying due to climate change, innovative solutions are emerging to predict and mitigate these disasters. One such advancement is the Probability of Fire (PoF) model developed by the European Centre for Medium-Range Weather Forecasts. This AI-driven system analyzes a multitude of factors, including weather conditions, vegetation dryness, and human activities, to forecast wildfire ignition hotspots with greater precision than traditional methods.

The effectiveness of the PoF model was notably demonstrated during the January 2025 wildfires in Los Angeles. By accurately identifying areas at high risk, the model enabled authorities to allocate resources more efficiently and issue timely evacuation orders, thereby enhancing public safety and reducing environmental damage.

Complementing these predictive models are technologies like the ALERTCalifornia camera network. This system, comprising over 1,150 AI-equipped cameras, has successfully detected more than 1,200 fires, often outperforming human 911 callers in early detection. In one instance, the cameras identified a fire in an Orange County canyon at night, prompting a swift response that prevented significant damage

These advancements underscore the transformative potential of AI in wildfire management. By harnessing vast datasets and real-time monitoring, AI tools are empowering authorities to anticipate and respond to wildfires more effectively, ultimately safeguarding communities and ecosystems

56. Guardians of the Green: How AI and Indigenous Voices Are Saving the Forest

Illegal deforestation remains one of the greatest threats to our planet. Forests, often called the lungs of the Earth, are rapidly vanishing due to unauthorized logging, mining, and agricultural expansion. This destruction not only contributes significantly to climate change, but also decimates biodiversity and displaces indigenous communities whose lives and cultures are deeply intertwined with the land. For decades, monitoring efforts have struggled to keep pace, limited by the sheer scale and remoteness of forested regions.

But a quiet revolution is underway—powered by artificial intelligence and grassroots action.

At the heart of this revolution is *ForestLink*, a groundbreaking initiative by the Rainforest Foundation UK. It's not just a piece of software—it's a lifeline. ForestLink allows people living in the world's most remote rainforests to act as real-time guardians of their ecosystems. Using simple mobile phones equipped with offline capabilities and geolocation, local monitors can log and transmit data on illegal logging, mining, or land invasions. Even without an internet connection, the data is saved, uploaded when signal becomes available, and then processed through AI algorithms to detect patterns and generate alerts for authorities.

One inspiring example comes from Lourdes, an indigenous Asháninka woman in the Peruvian Amazon. With support from ForestLink, she and her community were able to document multiple incursions by illegal loggers deep in their ancestral territory. "Before, we had no voice," Lourdes told a field officer. "Now we have the tools to protect our forests, and our future."

Thanks to reports from communities like Lourdes', Peruvian authorities have intervened in areas where previously no data was available. In Cameroon and the Democratic Republic of Congo, similar success stories have unfolded—evidence that empowering local stewards with smart tools leads to real, lasting change.

ForestLink is more than an app—it's a model of what happens when local knowledge meets cutting-edge technology. It turns passive observation into empowered action, and makes forest defenders out of everyday people. By combining AI, data transparency, and human courage, it's reshaping the fight against deforestation from the ground up.

57. Grid Awakening: AI's Role in the Future of Urban Sustainability

Cities are the beating hearts of modern civilization—but they're also voracious consumers of energy. As urban populations swell, the pressure on aging grids and fossil-fuel-reliant systems grows more intense. The dream of sustainable, efficient, and responsive cities can often feel like a distant reality. But thanks to artificial intelligence, that dream is starting to take shape.

In a model city dubbed EcoVille, leaders took bold steps to address the twin crises of energy inefficiency and climate change. Their answer was *SmartGrid AI*, an advanced energy management platform built to rethink how cities use and share electricity. This AI-powered system monitors real-time data from across the city—energy demand, solar and wind generation, temperature shifts, and even traffic patterns—to dynamically balance energy distribution. It doesn't just react; it predicts.

One of the biggest game-changers? Residents are part of the system. Through user-friendly apps, they receive tailored suggestions—like shifting laundry or charging electric vehicles during off-peak hours. These small actions, when adopted city-wide, create a ripple effect of change.

The results were transformative: within the first year, EcoVille saw a 20% drop in total energy consumption and a 30% boost in the effective use of renewable energy. Carbon emissions fell. Residents saw noticeable savings on utility bills. And critically, the grid became more resilient to outages and demand surges.

This isn't just theory. A similar real-world story is unfolding in Fremont, California, where GreenCom Networks, a European smart energy company, partnered with city planners to pilot AI-based grid management. One resident, Mark, a tech-savvy homeowner with rooftop solar, saw firsthand how his energy use changed. "It's like my house became part of something bigger. I didn't have to change much—but suddenly, I'm saving more and helping the grid," he said in an interview with *Energy Digital*.

With AI systems like SmartGrid, cities are learning to think—and act—smarter. These systems don't just cut waste; they build awareness, reduce dependence on fossil fuels, and bring citizens into the sustainability journey.

EcoVille might be fictional, but the blueprint it represents is very real—and already taking root in cities worldwide.

Mobility & Transportation

"A developed country is not a place where the poor have cars. It's where the rich use public transportation." — Enrique Peñalosa, former Mayor of Bogotá

Innovative technologies are reshaping urban mobility, driving smarter traffic management, faster and more efficient delivery services, and greener transportation solutions. By harnessing vast amounts of data and real-time analytics, these systems are helping cities reduce congestion, lower emissions, and improve quality of life. This section features three case studies that illustrate how intelligent tools are redefining the future of urban transportation.

58. Red Lights to Green Futures: AI and the Commute Revolution in Los Angeles

Urban traffic isn't just a daily frustration—it's a silent crisis. Congested roads mean lost hours, heightened stress, and a surge in carbon emissions that choke our cities. For decades, cities like Los Angeles have wrestled with traffic snarls that seem immune to every conventional solution.

But now, artificial intelligence is changing the rules of the road.

To tackle its legendary gridlock, Los Angeles launched the ATSAC system—short for *Automated Traffic Surveillance and Control*. Originally developed during the 1984 Olympics, it has evolved into one of the most advanced AI-powered traffic management systems in the world. At its core, ATSAC uses real-time data from over 5,000 traffic signal intersections, combined with traffic cameras, sensors, and GPS data. Through machine learning, it predicts congestion patterns and dynamically adjusts traffic lights to ease the flow—not just in isolated spots but across entire corridors of the city.

The transformation has been tangible. According to the Los Angeles Department of Transportation, commute times on major corridors have dropped by up to 12%, with significant improvements in air quality thanks to reduced idling at intersections.

A real-life example of the impact comes from Carlos, a rideshare driver in East LA. "Before, I'd spend 8 hours a day driving and half of it felt like sitting still," he shared in a local interview. "Now, I get more rides in, less stress, and my gas bill has actually dropped. It's like someone turned the city into a living, thinking thing."

AI didn't just improve his route—it improved his livelihood.

What's inspiring is that LA's innovation is being watched by cities around the globe. From Jakarta to Johannesburg, planners are exploring how AI can not only reduce congestion, but reimagine cities as dynamic, responsive ecosystems where humans and technology move in sync.

It's a glimpse of what cities can become when they stop reacting to traffic—and start predicting it.

59. Sidewalks and Silicon: The Rise of Autonomous Delivery in Smart Cities

The surge in e-commerce has revolutionized how we shop—but it's also clogged our cities with delivery vans, delayed packages, and increased carbon emissions. The "last mile"—the final leg of a parcel's journey to a customer's doorstep—has become one of the most expensive and inefficient segments of logistics.

But in Singapore, the future of last-mile delivery is already rolling through the streets—one robot at a time.

To address this modern challenge, Singaporean tech company Advantech partnered with logistics providers to deploy a new fleet of autonomous delivery robots powered by its AIR-030 Edge AI Inference System. These robots are designed not just to deliver, but to *think*. Equipped with GPS, cameras, LIDAR, and AI algorithms, they navigate city sidewalks, pedestrian zones, and even crosswalks—adjusting in real-time to dynamic environments.

The impact was swift and impressive. According to a case study by Advantech, property managers and logistics partners reported faster, more consistent deliveries, especially within large residential complexes and office campuses. Operational costs dropped due to reduced fuel use and labor requirements, while the community benefited from quieter streets and fewer delivery trucks.

Liyana, a logistics coordinator at a major condo development in Singapore's Central District, described the transformation: "We used to get 100 parcels a day—couriers would crowd the lobby, residents complained, it was chaos. Now, the robots handle over half of those, quietly and efficiently. It feels like we're living in the future."

Singapore's pilot program is becoming a model for urban logistics worldwide. From Tokyo to Toronto, cities are exploring how edge AI and robotics can address both the growing demands of e-commerce and the sustainability goals of the 21st century.

These robots aren't replacing humans—they're redefining what smart cities look like: seamless, efficient, and sustainable.

60. From Idle to Impact: The AI Behind Cleaner, Faster Ride-Sharing

When ride-sharing first hit the streets, it felt like the future had arrived—on demand, affordable, and effortlessly convenient. But as millions embraced platforms like Uber, an unintended consequence emerged: more cars on the road, more miles driven, and more emissions pumped into the air. The very technology meant to solve urban congestion was beginning to contribute to it.

That's when Uber turned to artificial intelligence—not just to get people from point A to B faster, but to do so more responsibly.

Using advanced machine learning models, Uber now predicts rider demand in real time, optimizes which driver to send for each request, and calculates the most efficient routes based on constantly updating traffic data. Their AI system also dynamically adjusts pricing, encourages carpooling through Uber Pool, and identifies ideal staging areas for drivers—reducing downtime and miles driven without passengers.

The impact has been significant. According to Uber's own reports, AI-driven optimizations have reduced idle time for drivers by over 20% in key markets, while also slashing unnecessary fuel consumption. And the more riders choose shared rides, the more the algorithm learns how to improve environmental efficiency across the network.

One real-life example is Maya, a driver in Austin, Texas, who saw a tangible shift after AI features were introduced. "I used to drive around waiting for a ping," she said in an interview with *The Verge*. "Now the app tells me where to go before someone even requests a ride. I make more money, and I use less gas. It's a win-win."

Uber's efforts are part of a broader transformation: using data not just to power profits, but to shape a greener, more sustainable future for mobility. By redesigning how we move—one optimized ride at a time—AI is helping cities breathe easier and move smarter.

Legal & Justice Systems

"Injustice anywhere is a threat to justice everywhere." — Martin Luther King Jr.

Technology is transforming the legal and justice systems by streamlining casework, uncovering hidden fraud, and helping to right past wrongs. From supporting overburdened public defenders to detecting inconsistencies in legal documents and aiding in the exoneration of the wrongfully convicted, these innovations are advancing access to justice, accuracy, and fairness. This section presents three compelling case studies that showcase how these tools are driving meaningful change in the pursuit of justice.

61. Justice at the Speed of AI: How Tech is Empowering Public Defenders

In the U.S. justice system, public defenders are often the unsung heroes—fighting to protect the rights of society's most vulnerable. Yet across the country, they're drowning under caseloads so heavy that meaningful, individualized legal representation can feel like a luxury. In Los Angeles County, where public defenders handle hundreds of thousands of cases annually, the challenge was particularly dire.

That's when the office turned to artificial intelligence—not to replace lawyers, but to *free* them.

In partnership with Amazon Web Services (AWS), the Los Angeles County Public Defender's Office implemented a groundbreaking AI-powered client case management system. This system, rooted in cloud-based machine learning, automates tedious document processing, eliminating up to 85% of manual data entry. It intelligently scans and indexes thousands of legal filings, makes them searchable by case and keyword, and alerts attorneys to new developments—often in real time.

The result is a dramatically more efficient legal workflow. Attorneys can now spend less time buried in paperwork and more time on what matters: strategy, client meetings, and courtroom advocacy.

One such attorney is Jessica, a veteran public defender who works primarily with low-income juveniles. "Before the AI system, I was spending hours a day sorting files, trying to track court notices and stay ahead of last-minute updates," she said in an interview with *Government Technology Magazine*. "Now, my dashboard tells me instantly when something new drops on a case. I can focus on fighting for my clients, not hunting down paperwork."

This transformation doesn't just improve productivity—it restores dignity to the defense process. When overburdened public defenders are empowered with real-time insights and automation, the legal system becomes more equitable and responsive. Justice, often slow and inaccessible, starts to move faster and reach farther.

The story of Los Angeles County's public defenders is a powerful example of AI not as a force of disruption—but as a force of support. It's not replacing human judgment, empathy, or advocacy. It's *amplifying* them.

62. Behind the Signature: How JPMorgan's AI Is Defending Trust in Finance

In the world of finance, trust is everything. Every loan agreement, every contract, every signature represents not just dollars—but reputations, livelihoods, and futures. Yet within the maze of legal documents that financial institutions manage daily, fraud can hide in plain sight—buried in fine print, masked by subtle inconsistencies, or forged beneath layers of bureaucracy.

At JPMorgan Chase, one of the world's largest and most scrutinized financial institutions, the stakes are too high to leave anything to chance. That's why they turned to artificial intelligence—not to simply speed up processes, but to protect the very foundation of trust.

Enter COiN, short for Contract Intelligence—an AI-powered platform developed by JPMorgan's internal technology team. Using machine learning algorithms, COiN rapidly scans and analyzes millions of legal documents, from credit agreements to commercial contracts. It extracts key data points, compares them to expected patterns, and flags anything that seems suspicious—often in seconds.

Before COiN, it would take legal teams approximately 360,000 hours annually to manually review these documents. Now, with AI assistance, that same workload is completed in mere minutes—saving time, reducing costs, and dramatically minimizing the risk of human error.

A real-world example comes from Sophia, a compliance officer at JPMorgan who was part of the early rollout. "Before COiN, we had a team of attorneys combing through contracts page by page," she explained in a profile published by *Business Insider*. "Now, we can catch red flags that we never would've noticed. It's not about replacing people—it's about giving them superpowers."

COiN has already prevented potentially damaging fraud attempts by identifying altered clauses in contracts—details that could have led to significant financial exposure. But more than that, it's helped redefine how financial institutions think about risk and responsibility.

By embracing AI not as a crutch but as a co-pilot, JPMorgan Chase is setting a new industry standard: one where ethics, efficiency, and intelligence work hand-in-hand to build a safer financial system.

63. Proof of Innocence: How AI Is Rewriting the Stories of the Wrongfully Convicted

For those wrongfully imprisoned, time is both the enemy and the evidence. Each passing day in a prison cell is a day stolen from a life that was never meant to be confined. For decades, advocates and legal teams have combed through boxes of evidence, battling bureaucratic inertia and outdated systems in their pursuit of justice. But now, something extraordinary is helping accelerate that pursuit: artificial intelligence.

At the California Innocence Project (CIP), a nonprofit dedicated to overturning wrongful convictions, AI has become a transformative ally. Leveraging advanced machine learning and generative AI tools, CIP can now analyze decades-old case files, transcripts, DNA test results, and police reports in a fraction of the time it once took. These systems are trained to recognize inconsistencies, detect language patterns that signal false confessions or coercion, and even suggest leads missed during the original investigations.

The results have been extraordinary—and for some, life-changing.

Gordon Cordeiro, convicted of murder in 1990, had long maintained his innocence. But the complexity of his case and the lack of resources delayed any meaningful review. It wasn't until CIP integrated AI-assisted evidence analysis that new DNA evidence was re-examined—ultimately proving Gordon had nothing to do with the crime. In 2023, after 30 years of wrongful incarceration, he was exonerated and walked free.

"AI didn't just read old files—it helped us *see them differently*," said Justin, a CIP case manager, in an interview with *NBC News*. "It connected dots we may have never seen and gave us a second chance to make things right."

Gordon's story is just one of many. The use of AI at CIP has since accelerated reviews in dozens of cases, providing a crucial advantage in situations where time, memory, and evidence have faded. The goal isn't to replace human judgment, but to augment it—to shine a light into the dark corners of justice where innocent people have been forgotten.

More than a tool, AI in this context becomes a force for redemption. It gives voice to those silenced and restores hope where it once seemed lost.

Journalism & Truth-Seeking

"Whoever controls the media, controls the mind." — Jim Morrison

Journalism is entering a new era of accuracy, speed, and insight as advanced tools help detect misinformation, automate transcription, and reveal hidden narratives within complex datasets. These innovations are empowering journalists to work more efficiently and uncover deeper truths, strengthening the integrity and impact of modern reporting. This section highlights three compelling case studies that showcase these breakthroughs in action.

64. Truth Machines: How AI Is Defending Democracy in the Age of Disinformation

In an age where misinformation spreads faster than facts, the truth has never been more fragile—or more vital. Nowhere is this more apparent than during elections, where the very fabric of democracy hinges on an informed public making decisions based on reality, not manipulation.

The rise of generative AI and deepfake technology has only intensified this challenge. Fabricated videos, doctored headlines, and AI-written news articles can mimic legitimacy so well that even seasoned readers are fooled. In response, a new ally has emerged in the fight to defend truth: artificial intelligence itself.

One of the most innovative efforts comes from Logically, a UK-based company that has partnered with democratic governments and fact-checking organizations globally to deploy AI systems that detect and flag disinformation—especially during election cycles. Logically's AI analyzes vast volumes of online content in real time, across platforms like Twitter (X), YouTube, Facebook, and Telegram. The system looks for anomalies in how posts spread, checks linguistic patterns, compares claims to verified data, and uses credibility scores to flag potential disinformation for human review.

This technology played a critical role during the 2022 Philippines presidential election, where misinformation campaigns ran rampant on social media. Maria, a journalist with a local watchdog group, recalled seeing deepfake videos that portrayed candidates making false or inflammatory statements. "They were so convincing," she said. "People were sharing them like wildfire. But with Logically's AI tools, we were able to trace the origin and prove it was fake before it did more harm."

Logically's efforts helped local fact-checkers flag over 1,000 false or misleading election-related posts, many of which would have otherwise gone viral. By combining automation with human expertise, they restored an essential layer of transparency at a time when the truth was under siege.

Today, similar systems are being deployed in India, the U.S., and across Europe ahead of major elections. These tools don't just filter lies—they help rebuild trust in information, ensuring that democracies are powered by knowledge rather than deception.

The war on disinformation isn't over, but AI is proving to be one of the most powerful tools in the defense of democratic truth.

65. AI Transcribes Breaking News in Real-Time

In the adrenaline-fueled world of breaking news, every second counts. The difference between being first or forgotten often comes down to speed—not just of speech, but of transcription, verification, and publication. For decades, journalists had to rely on fast typing, late nights, and hours of rewinding audio to capture the exact quotes that could shape a headline or define a crisis.

Today, thanks to artificial intelligence, that bottleneck has all but vanished.

Newsrooms around the world have embraced AI-powered transcription tools to keep pace with the modern news cycle. These systems, powered by companies like Otter.ai, Trint, and Rev AI, use real-time speech recognition and natural language processing to transcribe interviews, press conferences, and live broadcasts with astonishing speed and accuracy. With support for multiple languages, speaker identification, and automatic punctuation, these tools allow journalists to focus less on typing and more on truth-telling.

During the 2022 U.S. midterm elections, national broadcasters like NPR and CBS News deployed Otter.ai to transcribe live debates and press briefings. Rachel, a political reporter with a regional news outlet in Pennsylvania, described the shift: "I used to spend hours after every debate just transcribing clips. Now, I have a full transcript in minutes. I can highlight key moments, fact-check quotes on the spot, and hit publish while the story's still unfolding."

Beyond speed, these tools are reshaping how news is crafted. By automating transcription, reporters can focus on deeper storytelling, rigorous analysis, and building trust with their audience. Accuracy improves because AI doesn't fatigue, and accessibility increases when transcripts are quickly made available to readers with hearing impairments or non-native speakers.

In an era where information moves at lightning speed, and misinformation often races ahead, AI transcription tools empower journalists to keep up—not just faster, but smarter. They are no longer just witnesses to history; they're interpreting it in real time, with the help of machines that never miss a word.

66. Investigative Journalists Use AI to Uncover Hidden Patterns

At the heart of investigative journalism lies one core mission: to uncover the truth—no matter how deeply buried it may be. In an era where corruption hides behind complex financial networks and global scandals are hidden in terabytes of data, the tools of journalism are evolving. And artificial intelligence is fast becoming one of its most powerful allies.

The International Consortium of Investigative Journalists (ICIJ) has pioneered the use of AI to examine some of the largest and most intricate data leaks in history. From the Panama Papers to the Pandora Papers, ICIJ has faced the monumental challenge of sorting through millions of documents, emails, PDFs, and spreadsheets. These are the raw materials of scandal—but only if you know where to look.

Enter AI.

ICIJ partnered with data scientists and developers to build Datashare, an open-source document analysis platform. Using machine learning algorithms, entity recognition, and pattern detection, the platform enables journalists to search across vast datasets, automatically identifying connections between individuals, companies, and financial records. AI flags anomalies, recognizes aliases, and maps out hidden networks faster than any human team ever could.

A powerful example of this technology at work came during the Pandora Papers investigation in 2021. Will Fitzgibbon, a senior reporter with ICIJ, described how AI-driven tools helped them uncover a network of offshore holdings tied to global leaders and billionaires. "We simply couldn't have made these discoveries manually," he said in an interview with *MIT Technology Review*. "AI gave us the power to scale our curiosity."

The result? One of the largest journalistic collaborations in history, involving over 600 reporters in 117 countries—and revelations that triggered resignations, reforms, and global investigations.

By weaving AI into their process, investigative journalists are no longer overwhelmed by the data deluge—they're empowered by it. Technology isn't replacing their instinct or ethics; it's amplifying their reach, sharpening their insights, and accelerating their impact.

In the age of information overload, AI is helping journalism fulfill its highest calling: to speak truth to power.

Nonprofits & Social Good

"The test of our progress is not whether we add more to the abundance of those who have much—it is whether we provide enough for those who have too little." — Franklin D. Roosevelt

Nonprofits and humanitarian organizations are leveraging cutting-edge technology to tackle some of the world's most pressing challenges—mapping poverty with precision, translating vital information during crises, and coordinating disaster responses with greater speed and accuracy. This section presents three compelling case studies that reveal how these innovations are driving meaningful change and saving lives on a global scale.

67. Pixels and Poverty: The Satellite Revolution in Humanitarian Aid

Poverty wears many faces—and too often, it remains invisible in the places where it matters most. In remote villages, post-conflict regions, or underserved rural areas, outdated or missing data can mean the difference between receiving aid and being forgotten. For decades, governments and NGOs have relied on household surveys to measure poverty—but these efforts are costly, slow, and difficult to scale across regions where infrastructure or security is lacking.

That's where artificial intelligence is changing the game—not just by automating analysis, but by illuminating the unseen.

A pioneering collaboration between Stanford University, World Bank, and NGOs including GiveDirectly and The Red Cross has led to a transformative breakthrough in AI-powered poverty mapping. Researchers at Stanford's SustainLab and Data for Development Lab developed machine learning models that analyze high-resolution satellite imagery to detect visual indicators of wealth and deprivation. These indicators—such as roof materials, crop density, road access, and building size—are processed and matched with existing field data to generate predictive poverty scores, even in areas that have never been surveyed.

A key figure in this breakthrough is Neal Jean, a Stanford Ph.D. researcher and co-author of the 2016 landmark paper, "Combining Satellite Imagery and Machine Learning to Predict Poverty," published in *Science*. "Our model can accurately estimate economic well-being in areas where we previously had no data," Jean explained. "It gives governments and NGOs a way to reach communities that have long been off the radar."

The impact is already tangible. In Uganda, the Red Cross used AI-generated poverty maps to guide its distribution of anti-malarial bed nets. Rather than relying on limited survey data, they targeted areas with the highest indicators of need—ensuring that resources reached the most vulnerable households first. This precision not only saved money and time but also saved lives.

For frontline workers like Amina, a community health volunteer in rural Northern Uganda, the difference was night and day. "Before, we didn't always know where help was needed most," she told a Red Cross field officer. "Now, the maps show us. It's like someone turned the lights on."

By turning pixels into insight and images into action, AI is giving humanitarian efforts a sharper lens and a wider reach. It's enabling compassion to be not just heartfelt—but highly targeted, efficient, and informed.

This is what happens when innovation meets empathy: data becomes dignity.

68. AI Translates Emergency Information into Local Dialects

In moments of crisis, seconds can save lives—but only if the message is understood.

During wildfires, floods, hurricanes, and public health emergencies, governments must communicate quickly and clearly. Yet in many multilingual communities, a life-saving alert in the wrong language can be as dangerous as silence. Words meant to protect can become meaningless noise—unless translated and delivered in a way people can understand and act upon.

That's where artificial intelligence is stepping in—not as a replacement for human responders, but as a bridge across linguistic divides.

AI-powered Natural Language Processing (NLP) systems are transforming emergency response communications around the world. These systems can ingest an official warning—like a flash flood alert or an evacuation order—and within seconds, translate it into dozens of local languages and dialects. Unlike generic translation apps, these tools are context-aware: they understand urgency, tone, and cultural nuance. Once translated, the messages are instantly pushed out via SMS, radio, social media, and even voice broadcasts—ensuring that no one is left behind simply because of the language they speak.

One compelling example comes from California's Office of Emergency Services (Cal OES), which began piloting AI-powered multilingual alert systems in 2021. The program partnered with Google's AI division and Transcend.io, a civic tech company, to help deliver wildfire evacuation alerts in over 20 languages, including Mixteco and Hmong—languages often spoken by migrant farmworker communities in high-risk zones.

Elena, a community health worker in Fresno County, witnessed the impact firsthand during the 2022 Oak Fire. "The last time we had a big fire, some of the families didn't leave until it was almost too late," she told *NPR*. "This time, they got a message in Mixteco on their phone—and they listened. That message saved lives."

By combining machine learning with linguistic equity, these systems go beyond efficiency—they restore trust. When people see their language reflected in life-saving information, they feel seen. And when disaster strikes, feeling seen can mean survival.

AI-powered translation is not just a technological upgrade. It's a human rights innovation. In a world shaped by diversity and risk, it's helping ensure that no voice is unheard—and no life is left unprotected.

69. Disaster Response Coordinated Through AI Algorithms

When disaster strikes, every minute matters—and every decision can mean the difference between chaos and coordination, survival and loss. From wildfires to hurricanes, emergency responders often face an overwhelming flood of incoming data: road closures, weather shifts, infrastructure failures, and desperate cries for help.

For years, sorting through this information in real time was nearly impossible. But with artificial intelligence, responders now have a tool that doesn't just track the storm—it thinks ahead of it.

AI-powered platforms are transforming disaster response around the globe. These systems ingest real-time data from satellites, IoT sensors, social media feeds, traffic cameras, and even 911 calls. Machine learning algorithms analyze this incoming stream to detect patterns, predict threats, and prioritize response actions. In some platforms—like One Concern, IBM's Weather Company, and the DARPA-supported Geospatial Cloud Analytics platform—reinforcement learning helps systems get smarter with each emergency, adapting their recommendations based on past performance and real-time developments.

During Hurricane Ian in 2022, emergency management teams in Florida used AI models to predict flood zones and storm surge areas down to the neighborhood level. This allowed FEMA and local agencies to issue targeted evacuation notices and pre-position supplies days in advance. One of those agencies partnered with One Concern, an AI company that provides predictive disaster modeling. The platform's real-time simulations helped planners see not just what was happening—but what was about to happen.

Angela, a logistics coordinator with the Florida Division of Emergency Management, described how AI changed her team's response. "We used to rely on static models and best guesses," she told *Reuters*. "Now, we get a real-time picture of where to send people, trucks, and supplies—sometimes even before the damage starts."

AI didn't just help mitigate damage. It helped *orchestrate* a faster, smarter, and more unified response across dozens of jurisdictions. NGOs, fire departments, state and federal agencies all synced to a shared dashboard that cut through the noise and focused efforts where they mattered most.

These innovations are a testament to what happens when cutting-edge technology meets frontline humanity. AI doesn't replace human responders—it equips them with the clarity, speed, and foresight needed to save lives.

As disasters grow more frequent and complex, AI is becoming not just a helpful assistant—but a critical partner in resilience.

Sports & Performance

"It's not the will to win that matters—everyone has that. It's the will to prepare to win that matters." — Paul "Bear" Bryant

Technology is reshaping the sports and fitness industries by unlocking new levels of performance, strategy, and personalization. From optimizing athlete training and predicting opponents' moves to delivering tailored coaching experiences for everyday fitness enthusiasts, these innovations are driving excellence on and off the field. This section highlights three inspiring case studies that showcase how data-driven insights are redefining the future of sports and wellness.

70. Code, Sweat, and Precision: Unlocking Peak Performance with AI-Powered Biomechanics

In elite sports, the difference between victory and injury can be measured in fractions of a second, or the smallest shift in posture. Yet for decades, athletes and coaches have relied on subjective methods—video review, stopwatch timing, and a coach's trained eye—to analyze technique and form. These methods, though valuable, often miss micro-movements that lead to fatigue, inefficiency, or injury.

Now, AI is stepping in—not to replace coaches, but to elevate the precision of performance and the power of prevention.

One breakthrough example is the use of AI-enhanced wearable sensors, developed by companies like Plantiga, KINEXON, and Motus Global. These sensors, worn on the body or embedded in footwear, collect high-frequency biomechanical data such as ground reaction force, gait patterns, joint angles, and muscle imbalances. The real magic lies in what happens next: AI algorithms analyze this flood of data in real time, flagging deviations from optimal movement patterns and offering actionable insights directly to an app.

One compelling story comes from Marquise Goodwin, an Olympic long jumper and NFL wide receiver who began using Plantiga's AI gait analytics after a string of lower-body injuries. "The insights I got were mind-blowing," he said in an interview with *ESPN*. "I could see exactly where my stride was breaking down. It gave me real feedback, not just a coach saying, 'run smoother.' It told me how."

Goodwin adjusted his stride mechanics and lower-body posture based on the AI's feedback, and in the following season, he returned with improved acceleration and no recurrence of soft-tissue injuries that had previously sidelined him.

For coaches and sports scientists, AI tools are becoming indispensable. They can track workload, monitor fatigue markers, and compare an athlete's current form with their baseline or even with elite performance models. Over time, the AI adapts—learning each athlete's unique biomechanics and providing personalized recommendations.

This fusion of data and intuition allows for a new kind of athletic development: one that emphasizes sustainable excellence. Athletes can now train harder and smarter, not just for their next competition, but for longer careers and healthier lives.

AI in form analysis isn't about perfection—it's about *potential*. It brings clarity to the invisible and empowers athletes to move through their sport—and their life—with greater power, purpose, and precision.

71. From Instinct to Insight: Real-Time Strategy Powered by AI on the Pitch

In the world of elite sports, success is often defined by seconds and centimeters. But behind every breathtaking goal or game-changing play lies something more elusive: *strategy*. Understanding an opponent's next move has always been one of the greatest challenges in competitive sports. Traditionally, it was the realm of experienced coaches with keen eyes, pouring over footage and relying on instinct. Now, artificial intelligence is stepping onto the pitch—not to replace that intuition, but to supercharge it.

One of the most striking applications of AI in sport comes from Zone7, a predictive analytics company that works with professional football (soccer) clubs across Europe. While Zone7 is best known for its injury prevention models, the same technology is being adapted to support real-time tactical strategy. Clubs use AI platforms to analyze thousands of data points—player positions, passing tendencies, formation shifts, and even weather conditions—to anticipate opponent behavior *as the game unfolds*.

A particularly compelling example occurred during the 2022 Major League Soccer season, where the Philadelphia Union integrated predictive AI from Second Spectrum, a tech firm partnered with both MLS and the NBA. During a match against a high-pressing rival, the Union's coaching staff received live insights showing early indicators of a change in pressing strategy. Using these AI-generated predictions, the coaching team altered their own midfield positioning and introduced a substitution two minutes before the opposition made its tactical shift.

Jim, the Union's head coach, described it as "one of those moments where data confirmed what our eyes suspected—but faster and with more certainty."

The results? A more fluid counterattack, control regained in midfield, and a goal that sealed the win.

AI doesn't just feed statistics—it learns from the unique rhythm of a match, comparing it against vast historical libraries of game scenarios to project what might happen next. Through real-time dashboards and custom alerts, coaches and analysts are equipped with a second set of eyes—ones that never blink and never forget.

Players benefit too. With post-match analysis now augmented by AI breakdowns, they gain deeper understanding of not only their movements but also their opponents' intentions. The result is smarter gameplay, faster decision-making, and more strategic adaptability on the field.

In this new era of sport, AI doesn't undermine the art of coaching—it elevates it. The coach's gut feeling now has a partner in precision. And the players? They're not just reacting to the game—they're anticipating it, play by play.

72. Your Pocket Coach: How AI Is Breaking Barriers in Personal Fitness

For millions of people, the desire to get fit comes with barriers: expensive gym memberships, busy schedules, and the cost or inaccessibility of personal trainers. But what if the guidance of a coach—complete with personalized plans, form correction, and progress tracking—could live in your pocket?

Thanks to artificial intelligence, it can.

AI-powered virtual coaches are redefining fitness for the digital age. These smart systems combine computer vision, machine learning, and real-time feedback loops to create a dynamic, personalized workout experience—accessible to anyone with a smartphone or webcam. Using your device's camera, these applications monitor posture, joint angles, and motion to guide your form as you move. When a squat is too shallow, the AI corrects you. When your back arches during a plank, it speaks up. It's like having a watchful coach by your side—only it never sleeps, and it adapts to *you*.

One standout example is Tempo, a smart home fitness system that uses 3D sensors and AI to provide instant feedback on form, suggest modifications based on fatigue or injury risk, and evolve your routine based on progress. Tempo has been credited by thousands for helping them build confidence and consistency—especially in isolated or underserved communities.

Rashida, a 42-year-old nurse and mother of three in Detroit, shared how Tempo transformed her post-pandemic routine. "I couldn't afford a personal trainer, and I didn't feel comfortable going back to the gym," she told *TechCrunch*. "Tempo became my coach. It corrected my form, kept me motivated, and I lost 20 pounds without ever leaving my living room."

Other popular apps like Freeletics, Fitbod, and Nike Training Club now integrate AI personalization to tailor workouts to your fitness level, mood, and available time. These platforms often evolve with user data, learning not just how your body moves—but how your habits shift over time.

The impact goes far beyond aesthetics. AI virtual coaches are democratizing fitness—removing financial, physical, and social barriers. For beginners afraid to start, or individuals managing chronic conditions, these tools offer encouragement without judgment, and guidance without pressure.

This isn't just a trend—it's a movement. One where the gym is wherever you are. Where a coach can fit in your pocket. And where health, strength, and confidence are just one algorithm away.

Business Operations

"It is not the strongest of the species that survives, nor the most intelligent, but the one most responsive to change." — Charles Darwin

Innovative technologies are transforming how businesses operate, streamlining processes, elevating customer experiences, and empowering smarter decision-making. From automating customer support to optimizing supply chains and revolutionizing recruitment, organizations across sectors are embracing intelligent solutions to work faster, serve better, and grow stronger. This section explores three powerful case studies that reveal how forward-thinking companies are reimagining the future of work.

73. Always On, Always Listening: How AI Chatbots Are Redefining Customer Care

In an era where instant gratification defines customer expectations, businesses are racing to meet the demand for fast, friendly, and flawless service. Gone are the days of long hold times and overflowing email inboxes. Today, help often comes in the form of a digital conversation—swift, smart, and always online.

Welcome to the age of AI-powered customer service.

Across industries, companies are embracing AI-driven chatbots to reshape how they interact with customers. These virtual assistants, powered by natural language processing (NLP) and machine learning, are capable of holding human-like conversations, resolving issues, and even predicting customer needs based on historical data. Whether it's helping reset a password, tracking a package, or guiding users through a product upgrade, AI chatbots are quickly becoming the frontline heroes of modern customer service.

One powerful example is Vodafone, a global telecommunications leader, which launched its AI chatbot, TOBi, to handle customer support across multiple regions. TOBi can understand and respond to a range of inquiries—billing, tech support, plan upgrades—24/7 and in several languages. Trained on millions of historical conversations, TOBi has achieved impressive results: resolving over 70% of customer queries without human assistance, reducing support costs, and improving customer satisfaction ratings.

Daniela, a customer service team lead at Vodafone Germany, described the shift this way: "TOBi doesn't replace us—it empowers us. We now have more time to focus on customers who really need that human touch, because TOBi takes care of everything else."

Building a chatbot like TOBi doesn't happen overnight. It begins with data collection and training, feeding the AI system with previous customer interactions, product FAQs, and resolution outcomes. The system then goes through integration with CRM platforms to retrieve and update live customer data in real time. Finally, the chatbot is fine-tuned through extensive testing and continuous learning, adapting to new questions and feedback over time.

The results have been transformative. Businesses deploying chatbots report faster response times, lower support costs, and higher customer satisfaction. Human agents are no longer bogged down with repetitive queries—they're free to resolve complex cases, strategize, and create deeper connections with customers.

More than just a support tool, AI chatbots are becoming strategic assets. They provide rich, real-time insights into customer behavior, preferences, and pain points—data that feeds back into product development, marketing, and service design.

Ultimately, this is not just a story of automation—it's a story of elevation. By handling the predictable, AI makes room for the exceptional. And in doing so, it's redefining what exceptional customer service looks like.

74. The Neural Network of Commerce: How AI Keeps the Global Supply Chain in Motion

The global economy runs on invisible highways—supply chains that connect ideas to production, warehouses to homes, and companies to customers. But these vast networks are more vulnerable than ever, facing disruptions from geopolitical shifts, pandemics, labor shortages, and unpredictable weather. In such a high-stakes environment, businesses are turning to artificial intelligence not just to survive—but to thrive.

Few companies illustrate this transformation better than Amazon, whose supply chain is often considered a benchmark in operational excellence. Behind the scenes, Amazon's use of AI and machine learning has revolutionized how products move across continents and into customers' hands—sometimes within hours.

At the heart of this innovation is Amazon's forecasting and optimization engine, which continuously digests vast streams of data: past sales, product reviews, seasonal trends, shipping routes, warehouse capacity, supplier timelines, and even external disruptions like hurricanes or port delays. Using this data, AI models make millions of real-time predictions—from how many phone chargers will sell in Dallas next Tuesday, to which delivery route will avoid a snowstorm and reach your doorstep faster.

One powerful example of this came during the COVID-19 pandemic, when global supply chains were thrown into chaos. Priya, an Amazon supply chain analyst based in Seattle, was part of the team using AI tools to adapt inventory flows as demand for home essentials surged. "We saw toilet paper, cleaning supplies, and fitness gear spike overnight," she told *Bloomberg*. "Our models helped us quickly shift fulfillment priorities and reroute shipments to meet demand. Without AI, we would've been flying blind."

Amazon's AI-powered demand forecasting reduced product shortages by over 20% during peak pandemic months, while its route optimization systems helped decrease delivery times and fuel consumption. Through real-time monitoring, the company could proactively respond to bottlenecks and adjust operations with precision.

The impact goes beyond just logistics. With faster deliveries, fewer stockouts, and greater operational agility, customer satisfaction has soared. At the same time, AI has helped Amazon cut waste, reduce emissions, and improve its environmental footprint—proving that what's good for efficiency can also be good for the planet.

In the age of digital commerce, AI isn't just managing the supply chain. It *is* the supply chain's central nervous system—coordinating, learning, and adapting at every link to meet the future, one delivery at a time.

75. Beyond the Resume: How AI Is Opening Doors to Fairer Hiring

In every organization, talent is the foundation—and recruitment is the gateway. Yet for decades, that gateway has too often been filtered through unconscious biases and outdated processes. Resumes judged on names rather than skill. Interviews that reward familiarity over potential. In the search for the best, many great candidates have been overlooked.

Enter artificial intelligence, not to replace the human touch, but to strengthen it with precision, fairness, and insight.

Across industries, AI-driven recruitment tools are being embraced to reimagine how companies find, evaluate, and hire talent. These systems are trained to read resumes, assess competencies, and identify matches based not on assumptions, but on *data*. Using natural language processing and predictive analytics, they can screen thousands of applicants in minutes—flagging those whose experience, skills, and potential align most closely with job requirements.

Take the case of Unilever, one of the world's largest consumer goods companies. Faced with over 250,000 applications annually, Unilever implemented an AI hiring platform powered by Pymetrics and HireVue. Instead of relying solely on traditional resumes, applicants now complete a series of neuroscience-based games that measure cognitive, emotional, and behavioral traits. AI then compares those results to traits of high-performing employees in similar roles.

The impact was profound: Unilever cut its time-to-hire by 75%, increased the diversity of its interview pool by 16%, and saved over 100,000 hours of human recruiter time.

Lara, a young jobseeker from Cape Town, was one of the beneficiaries. "I didn't go to a big-name university, and I worried my resume wouldn't stand out," she said in an interview. "But through the games, I could show who I really was. I didn't need a connection—I just needed a chance." That chance led to her securing a full-time role in brand management.

The implementation of these systems involves more than plugging in algorithms. It starts with algorithm development, training AI models to evaluate candidates against fair and measurable job criteria. Then comes bias auditing, where companies work with ethicists, legal teams, and data scientists to regularly test systems for unintended bias. Finally, there's human oversight—the essential step where recruiters review AI insights, conduct interviews, and make the final hiring decisions, ensuring nuance and empathy remain part of the process.

This approach has not only improved efficiency and diversity, but also candidate experience. Real-time feedback, faster responses, and reduced anxiety about the "black hole" of application portals have made the journey more human—even when assisted by machines.

But make no mistake: AI is a *tool*, not a solution in itself. When used responsibly, it doesn't just speed up hiring—it *levels the playing field*. It empowers organizations to uncover hidden talent, to reach beyond the usual suspects, and to build teams that reflect the diverse world they serve.

In today's global talent landscape, the best candidates may not look like the last. AI helps ensure that the future of work starts with *fair opportunity*—and that brilliance isn't lost in the shuffle.

Marketing & Advertising

"You never get a second chance to make a first impression." — Will Rogers

Advanced technology is reshaping the marketing and advertising world, empowering brands to craft breakthrough campaigns, reach precisely defined audiences, and produce content that truly connects. Through three compelling case studies, this section reveals how data-driven creativity and intelligent automation are unlocking new levels of engagement, personalization, and performance in modern marketing.

76. Past Meets Power: The Virtual Match That Celebrated a Legend's Evolution

In the ever-evolving world of advertising, where attention is fleeting and authenticity is everything, brands face a constant challenge: how to connect in a way that feels *real*. Enter artificial intelligence—not just as a tool, but as a co-creator in storytelling. At the intersection of technology, sport, and emotion, Nike delivered one of the most innovative ad campaigns of the last decade, powered by AI and driven by greatness.

Titled "Never Done Evolving," the campaign honored Serena Williams, one of the most iconic athletes in history, by staging a virtual match between her 17-year-old self in 1999 and her 35-year-old self in 2017. The concept was bold: use AI to pit Serena against herself, showcasing not just her dominance, but her *transformation* over nearly two decades.

Nike partnered with creative agency Wieden+Kennedy and AKQA, along with AI company The Zone, to bring the campaign to life. Using hundreds of hours of match footage, biomechanical data, and shot analytics, AI models were trained to simulate Serena's playing style from both eras. The resulting match wasn't just visually realistic—it was emotionally compelling, revealing how much Serena had evolved in power, technique, strategy, and resilience.

"People always compare me to me," Serena said in a behind-the-scenes interview. "But I've never had a chance to actually see it that way."

The video—part animation, part data-driven simulation—was a viral success. It aired during the 2022 U.S. Open, just as Serena was making what many believed could be her final professional appearance. The timing, message, and execution were pitch-perfect. Viewers weren't just watching a game—they were witnessing a story of growth, perseverance, and legacy.

Beyond the spectacle, the campaign achieved what few tech-driven ads manage: emotional connection. It stirred reflection on how far we can come, how much we can change, and what it means to keep evolving—on the court, in business, in life.

Nike's "Never Done Evolving" wasn't just a campaign. It was a statement. A fusion of data and heart, showing that AI isn't just about precision—it can also be deeply human. By pairing technological innovation with a personal, almost spiritual narrative, Nike proved once again that it's not just in the business of selling shoes—it's in the business of *inspiration.*

77. Threading Intelligence: How a Gown Boutique Stitched AI Into Its Success Story

In the highly competitive world of fashion retail—especially in niche segments like prom and bridal—small businesses often face an uphill climb. Big brands dominate digital ad space, influencer partnerships are costly, and customer expectations for fast, personalized service are higher than ever. For many small companies, success hinges on one question: *How do we do more with less?*

For Amarra, a New Jersey-based boutique distributor of special-occasion gowns, the answer came from a surprising place—artificial intelligence.

Known for its elegant prom, pageant, and bridal collections, Amarra operates in a space where aesthetic precision and customer responsiveness are everything. But with a growing online presence and a constantly changing catalog, the team struggled to keep up with the demands of content creation, inventory planning, and customer service.

That changed when Amarra adopted a suite of AI-powered tools across its operations. With the help of ChatGPT, the team began generating detailed, on-brand product descriptions for hundreds of SKUs, cutting content creation time by over 60%. What once took a copywriter days could now be completed in hours—without sacrificing quality or tone.

Sarah, the head of e-commerce at Amarra, explained the impact. "We used to spend so much time crafting descriptions that we'd delay getting new dresses online. Now we can move faster and focus more on the visual storytelling and campaign planning that really drives engagement."

In parallel, Amarra introduced an AI-based inventory management system trained on historical sales data, seasonal trends, and color/style preferences. The result? A 40% drop in overstocking, more accurate reordering, and less capital tied up in unsold merchandise.

To round out the transformation, the team deployed an AI-driven chatbot on their site and social platforms. It now handles over 70% of customer queries, including sizing questions, order tracking, and return policies. That freed up Amarra's small customer service team to focus on high-touch cases like VIP client inquiries or boutique consultations.

Collectively, these tools allowed Amarra to level the playing field—not by outspending competitors, but by outsmarting them. The company now operates more efficiently, connects more meaningfully with customers, and can scale without hiring dozens of new staff. Perhaps most importantly, they've become a model for how small businesses can integrate AI thoughtfully to amplify their human creativity, not replace it.

For Amarra, AI wasn't about automating away the magic of fashion—it was about giving a passionate team the space and speed to focus on what matters most: creating unforgettable moments for their customers.

78. AI-Powered Copywriting Tools Enhance Landing Page Conversions

In the digital age, first impressions aren't made face-to-face—they're made on landing pages.

Whether it's a bold headline, a crisp product benefit, or a well-placed call-to-action, the quality of a landing page often determines whether a customer clicks *buy now* or closes the tab. But creating high-converting pages takes time, creativity, and a deep understanding of your audience. For many small businesses and marketers juggling a hundred tasks, that's a luxury they don't always have.

That's where artificial intelligence—and specifically, platforms like Copy.ai—is stepping in.

Launched in 2020, Copy.ai leverages natural language processing and machine learning to generate persuasive marketing content. Users simply input details about their product, audience, and tone of voice, and the AI produces tailored copy for everything from headlines and bullet points to full landing page paragraphs.

One real-world example comes from Geoffrey, a solo founder of a productivity startup called Taskable. As a non-writer trying to launch a SaaS product, Geoffrey struggled to create copy that converted visitors into sign-ups. "I was spending hours trying to write headlines that didn't feel right," he told *TechCrunch*. "Then I tried Copy.ai. Within minutes, I had 10 variations that actually sounded like something I'd want to click on."

Geoffrey reported a doubling of his conversion rate after switching to AI-generated copy, which allowed him to spend more time improving the product and less time sweating over text. He's not alone. Companies across e-commerce, SaaS, and online education are using Copy.ai to test multiple versions of their landing pages in record time—accelerating growth and reducing reliance on expensive copywriting resources.

The true innovation isn't just speed—it's *alignment*. Copy.ai's AI learns from thousands of high-performing examples and adapts to specific industries and styles, producing content that feels natural and on-brand. The result? High-performing pages that don't sound like they were written by a robot—and that drive results.

More than a writing tool, AI platforms like Copy.ai are enabling small teams to scale like large ones. They're giving solo entrepreneurs and marketers superpowers—to move faster, test bolder ideas, and communicate with clarity at scale.

The future of landing pages isn't less human—it's more *empowered*. Because when great ideas meet great execution, the clicks follow.

Design & Architecture

"We shape our buildings; thereafter they shape us." — Winston Churchill

New technologies are redefining design and architecture, unlocking unprecedented creativity, precision, and personalization. From generative algorithms that craft intricate architectural forms to digital twins that revolutionize urban planning and intelligent tools that tailor interior spaces to individual needs, professionals are transforming how they imagine and build the world around us. This section explores three powerful case studies that showcase this inspiring shift in the creative and built environment.

79. Generative Design Transforms Architectural Creativity

In the realm of contemporary architecture, the integration of AI-driven generative design tools has opened new avenues for creativity and complexity. A notable example is the work of Michael Hansmeyer, a Swiss architect renowned for his pioneering use of algorithms to create intricate and complex architectural forms.

Hansmeyer's project, *Subdivided Columns*, exemplifies the potential of generative design. By employing computational algorithms, he generated column designs with millions of unique facets, resulting in structures that are both highly detailed and structurally sound. These columns were fabricated using CNC milling techniques, translating digital designs into tangible architectural elements.

The generative process begins with a simple geometric form, which is then recursively subdivided according to specific algorithmic rules. This method allows for the exploration of a vast design space, producing forms that would be unimaginable through traditional design methods. The resulting columns exhibit a level of complexity and ornamentation reminiscent of natural forms, such as coral or crystalline structures.

Hansmeyer's work demonstrates how AI-driven generative design can push the boundaries of architectural creativity, enabling the creation of forms that are both innovative and feasible. By harnessing the power of algorithms, architects can explore a multitude of design possibilities, optimize structural performance, and achieve a harmonious balance between aesthetics and functionality.

80. AI Enhances Urban Planning and Design

The convergence of AI and urban planning holds significant promise for creating more intelligent, efficient, and sustainable cities. A prime example of this integration is the *Virtual Singapore* project, a dynamic three-dimensional (3D) city model and collaborative data platform developed by the Singaporean government.

Virtual Singapore serves as a digital twin of the city, allowing urban planners, architects, and policymakers to simulate and visualize various urban scenarios. The platform integrates data from multiple sources, including geographic information systems (GIS), real-time sensor data, and demographic information, to provide a comprehensive view of the urban environment.

One of the key applications of Virtual Singapore is in urban planning and design. Planners can use the platform to test the impact of new developments, infrastructure projects, and policy changes before implementation. For instance, they can simulate traffic flow, assess environmental impacts, and evaluate the effectiveness of proposed public spaces. This predictive capability enables more informed decision-making, leading to urban developments that are better aligned with sustainability goals and residents' needs.

Furthermore, Virtual Singapore facilitates public engagement by providing a visual and interactive means for citizens to understand and contribute to urban planning processes. Residents can explore proposed changes to their neighborhoods, provide feedback, and participate more actively in shaping their urban environment.

The success of Virtual Singapore underscores the transformative potential of AI in urban planning. By leveraging AI and data analytics, cities can become more responsive, resilient, and sustainable, ultimately enhancing the quality of life for their inhabitants.

81. AI-Driven Personalization in Interior Design

Artificial intelligence is making significant strides in the field of interior design, particularly in creating personalized and contextually relevant designs. A notable example is the work of *Not Quite Past*, a company that utilizes AI to generate bespoke tile designs inspired by historical styles.

Not Quite Past employs machine learning algorithms trained on a vast dataset of traditional tile patterns from various historical periods and cultures. Clients can input specific themes, motifs, or stylistic preferences, and the AI system generates unique tile designs that align with the provided criteria. This approach allows for a high degree of personalization, enabling clients to incorporate elements of historical artistry into contemporary spaces.

The AI-driven design process not only enhances aesthetic appeal but also streamlines production. Once a design is finalized, it can be directly translated into manufacturing instructions for tile production, reducing lead times and minimizing errors. Additionally, the system can optimize designs for material efficiency, contributing to more sustainable manufacturing practices.

Not Quite Past's innovative use of AI in interior design demonstrates the technology's potential to bridge the gap between historical art forms and modern personalization demands. By harnessing AI, designers can offer clients unique, customized solutions that honor traditional aesthetics while embracing contemporary technology.

Manufacturing & Industry

"If you can't measure it, you can't improve it."
— Peter Drucker

A new era of manufacturing and industrial innovation is unfolding, fueled by intelligent systems that boost efficiency, enhance safety, and accelerate creativity. From predictive maintenance that prevents costly downtime to smart robotics tackling dangerous tasks, and advanced 3D printing guided by data-driven materials design, technology is redefining what's possible on the factory floor and beyond. This section highlights three powerful case studies that capture this transformative shift in action.

82. The Silent Sentinel: How AI Is Preventing Downtime Before It Begins

In the high-stakes world of manufacturing, a single broken machine can bring a multimillion-dollar production line to a standstill. Downtime doesn't just cost money—it erodes trust, delays deliveries, and disrupts global supply chains. For manufacturers seeking to stay ahead, the question isn't whether to fix what's broken—it's how to see the break *before it happens*.

At Siemens, one of the world's leading industrial manufacturing giants, this challenge sparked a bold transformation. The company turned to artificial intelligence to move beyond traditional maintenance routines and into the era of predictive maintenance.

The strategy was simple in concept but revolutionary in execution. Siemens outfitted its production equipment with IoT sensors, which continuously monitored key indicators like temperature, vibration, pressure, and sound frequency. But raw data wasn't enough. Siemens partnered with data scientists and AI engineers to build machine learning models capable of detecting subtle anomalies—those invisible red flags that signal a potential failure weeks in advance.

The real magic? The AI wasn't just trained on theoretical data. It learned from Siemens' own historical maintenance logs, failure reports, and repair timelines—giving it a context-rich understanding of how each machine *behaves when it's healthy* versus when it's on the verge of a problem.

One of the champions of this transformation is Daniel, a predictive maintenance manager at Siemens' Amberg plant in Germany. "Before AI, our best-case scenario was scheduled maintenance. But that's still based on averages," he shared. "Now we can address issues before the machine even *knows* it's failing."

Instead of reacting to emergencies, Siemens teams now operate proactively, deploying technicians only when the AI flags something unusual. And because of this precision, the company's production lines run smoother, its machinery lasts longer, and its customers experience fewer delays.

This shift didn't just optimize machinery—it redefined the role of maintenance itself, turning it from a cost center into a strategic function. Siemens' success is now a beacon for manufacturers across the globe, proving that AI isn't a futuristic concept—it's an essential tool in building resilient, agile, and intelligent factories.

In an industry built on precision, predictive AI is becoming the most precise instrument of all—capable not only of diagnosing the present, but anticipating the future.

83. AI Robots Handle Dangerous Tasks with Precision

In industrial environments, tasks that involve exposure to hazardous materials, extreme temperatures, or repetitive motions pose significant risks to human workers. To mitigate these dangers, companies are increasingly deploying AI-powered robots designed to perform such tasks with high precision and reliability.

One notable example is the collaboration between BMW and Figure Robotics. BMW integrated Figure's humanoid robots into their production lines to handle strenuous and potentially dangerous tasks. These robots, standing at five feet six inches, are equipped with advanced cameras, sensors, and AI algorithms that enable them to navigate complex environments and perform tasks such as inserting sheet metal parts into assembly fixtures. The robots' human-like dexterity allows them to seamlessly integrate into existing manufacturing processes without extensive reconfiguration.

The introduction of these AI-powered robots led to a 400% increase in task execution speed and significantly improved precision in part placements. By taking over hazardous tasks, the robots reduced the risk of workplace injuries and allowed human workers to focus on more complex and strategic aspects of production. This not only enhanced overall productivity but also contributed to a safer and more efficient working environment.

This case highlights the growing role of AI and robotics in transforming industrial operations. By automating dangerous tasks, companies can protect their workforce, improve precision, and achieve higher efficiency, demonstrating the profound impact of AI-driven automation in modern manufacturing.

84. Smarter Machines, Stronger Materials: The Rise of AI-Driven Manufacturing

The convergence of artificial intelligence and 3D printing is forging a new frontier in materials science, unlocking unprecedented possibilities in design, production, and sustainability. What once took weeks of trial-and-error in traditional labs is now being accomplished in hours, thanks to machine learning models that not only learn from data—but actively reshape the future of manufacturing.

At the heart of this transformation is the work being done at *Arizona State University's* Advanced Manufacturing and Materials Processing (AMMP) lab. There, researchers have pioneered AI-powered software that fine-tunes the 3D printing process in real time. The result? Stronger, lighter, and more precisely engineered parts, printed faster and with less waste.

One shining example of this revolution in action is the journey of *Jared*, a doctoral student at ASU and one of the lead minds behind the AI tool. Jared's passion began in aerospace engineering, where he encountered the frustrating inefficiencies of traditional prototyping methods. Inspired by the possibilities of intelligent automation, he helped develop a neural network that analyzes real-time sensor data to adjust printer settings mid-process—adapting on the fly to ensure optimal layer adhesion, temperature control, and material deposition.

One tangible success from this work can be seen in aerospace applications. By using AI to optimize parameters for titanium alloys, the ASU team was able to produce aerospace brackets with a 25% weight reduction and a 30% increase in structural integrity. These improvements contribute directly to reduced fuel consumption—an innovation that has far-reaching implications for sustainable aviation.

Beyond aerospace, industries from automotive to healthcare are taking note. Whether it's custom orthopedic implants or lightweight car chassis, the AI-3D printing synergy is enabling mass customization with microscopic precision, reducing human error, and accelerating time-to-market.

This isn't just a step forward—it's a leap into the future of manufacturing, where intelligent machines co-create the materials of tomorrow.

Space & Frontiers

"Any sufficiently advanced technology is indistinguishable from magic." — Arthur C. Clarke

Artificial intelligence (AI) is revolutionizing space exploration, enabling unprecedented discoveries and enhancing mission efficiencies. From identifying distant exoplanets to navigating Martian terrain and ensuring the safety of private space ventures, AI's integration into space missions is opening new frontiers. This section delves into three compelling case studies that exemplify AI's transformative impact on space exploration.

85. Cosmic Codebreakers: Unveiling the Universe's Secrets with AI and Kepler

The quest to discover exoplanets—planets orbiting stars beyond our solar system—has been a cornerstone of modern astronomy. NASA's Kepler Space Telescope, launched in 2009, amassed a vast dataset, observing over 150,000 stars and capturing minute fluctuations in their brightness to identify potential exoplanet transits. However, the sheer volume of data presented a significant challenge: manually sifting through this information to pinpoint exoplanet candidates was both time-consuming and prone to human error.

In a groundbreaking collaboration, NASA partnered with Google to harness the power of artificial intelligence in analyzing Kepler's data. They employed a neural network—a type of machine learning algorithm inspired by the human brain's interconnected neuron structure—to automate the detection process. This neural network was trained using 15,000 previously vetted signals from Kepler's catalog, enabling it to distinguish between genuine exoplanet transits and false positives with remarkable accuracy.

The efficacy of this AI-driven approach became evident when it identified Kepler-90i, the eighth planet orbiting the Kepler-90 star, located over 2,500 light-years from Earth. This discovery was particularly significant as it marked the first time a star system with as many planets as our own solar system had been identified. The neural network's ability to detect such a subtle signal amidst the vast dataset underscored AI's potential in astronomical research.

Building on this success, NASA introduced ExoMiner, a more advanced machine learning algorithm designed to validate exoplanet candidates. Utilizing data from Kepler and its extended mission, K2, ExoMiner successfully confirmed 301 new exoplanets. Its design allows it to learn from existing data, making it adept at discerning real planets from false positives, thereby streamlining the validation process.

The integration of AI into exoplanet discovery has revolutionized the field, enabling the analysis of vast datasets with unprecedented speed and precision. This synergy between human expertise and machine learning accelerates the pace of discovery and enhances our understanding of the universe's diversity.

86. Smart Rovers, Bold Discoveries: The AI Revolution on Mars

Mars exploration has always been fraught with challenges, from unpredictable terrain to communication delays. Traditional rover operations required meticulous planning, with commands sent from Earth and executed after significant delays. This process limited the rovers' responsiveness and efficiency.

The Perseverance rover, which landed on Mars in February 2021, represents a paradigm shift in autonomous planetary exploration. Equipped with advanced AI systems, Perseverance can make real-time decisions about navigation and scientific investigations. Its Enhanced AutoNav system allows it to autonomously traverse the Martian surface, identifying and avoiding obstacles without direct input from mission control.

One of the standout AI tools onboard Perseverance is AEGIS (Autonomous Exploration for Gathering Increased Science). AEGIS enables the rover to analyze its surroundings and select scientifically valuable targets for study. For instance, when searching for specific rock compositions, AEGIS can process images, identify promising specimens, and direct the rover's instruments to conduct detailed analyses.

The integration of AI has markedly increased Perseverance's operational efficiency. According to NASA, the rover's ability to autonomously navigate and make scientific decisions has resulted in a 30% increase in the volume of data collected compared to previous missions. This autonomy not only accelerates the pace of exploration but also allows for more flexible and adaptive mission planning.

The success of AI in Mars exploration underscores its potential to revolutionize planetary missions. By reducing reliance on Earth-based commands and enabling real-time decision-making, AI empowers rovers to explore more ambitiously and efficiently, paving the way for future missions to venture deeper into our solar system.

87. Orbit Without Chaos: How AI is Guiding the Future of Satellite Safety

The burgeoning private space industry has introduced new challenges, particularly in satellite navigation and orbital safety. With thousands of satellites now orbiting Earth—and thousands more planned—our near-Earth environment has grown dangerously crowded. Every new launch adds complexity to an already chaotic orbital dance. One stray collision can create a cascade of debris, endangering future missions and billions of dollars in infrastructure. Managing that risk is no longer optional—it's mission critical.

Enter Kayhan Space, a Colorado-based aerospace software company leading the charge with AI-powered solutions. Their flagship product, Pathfinder, is designed to help satellite operators navigate the increasingly crowded space lanes with confidence. Using machine learning algorithms, Pathfinder analyzes satellite trajectories, predicts potential collisions with other spacecraft or debris, and recommends optimal maneuvers to avoid them—all in real time.

Unlike traditional space traffic management systems, which rely heavily on manual calculations and public data sources, Pathfinder integrates multiple data streams and uses proprietary AI models to identify potential risks days before traditional systems would catch them. The software can assess the probability of conjunctions, quantify risk levels, and even automate recommended actions for satellite operators. This proactive approach saves precious time—and potentially lives and assets.

One compelling example occurred in 2022 when a commercial satellite operator using Pathfinder was alerted to a high-risk conjunction with a piece of debris from a previous rocket launch. Thanks to the AI's early prediction, the satellite was repositioned with ample margin, avoiding not only a catastrophic loss but also a ripple effect of debris that could have threatened multiple other satellites. "We prevented what could've been a very serious situation," a company engineer stated. "The AI gave us a warning 48 hours before other systems flagged it."

Kayhan's impact is extending beyond safety. As space becomes more commercialized, AI tools like Pathfinder are helping operators optimize fuel usage, extend satellite lifespans, and reduce the need for human oversight. In a business where every maneuver costs fuel—and every delay costs money—AI offers a competitive edge.

The company has already partnered with major satellite operators and private space firms, including Spire Global and Capella Space. Even defense and government entities are taking notice. As low-Earth orbit (LEO) becomes a high-stakes arena for innovation and geopolitics, the ability to autonomously manage fleets of satellites safely will separate leaders from laggards.

AI's role in space isn't just about rockets and robots—it's about orchestration. Like an invisible conductor in a galactic symphony, AI ensures that satellites don't crash into each other, debris doesn't spiral out of control, and ambitious missions don't end in silence. For the private space industry, AI is quickly becoming the unsung hero keeping the cosmos open for business.

Farming & Food Systems

"The ultimate goal of farming is not the growing of crops, but the cultivation and perfection of human beings." — Masanobu Fukuoka, Japanese farmer and philosopher

From precision farming and early disease detection to autonomous machinery, cutting-edge technologies are transforming agriculture into a smarter, more sustainable industry. These innovations are helping farmers boost productivity, reduce waste, and safeguard food security in the face of growing global challenges. This section highlights three powerful case studies that showcase how intelligent systems are reshaping the future of farming.

88. Fields of Intelligence: How AI is Cultivating a Smarter, Greener Future for Farming

In the heart of the American Midwest, a region known as the "Corn Belt," farmers have long faced the challenge of optimizing crop yields while managing resources efficiently. Traditional farming methods often relied on uniform application of water, fertilizers, and pesticides across vast fields, leading to inefficiencies and environmental concerns. Enter Smart Farm Agritech, a pioneering agricultural technology company that has harnessed the power of AI to revolutionize precision farming.

Smart Farm Agritech developed an AI-driven platform that integrates data from various sources, including satellite imagery, soil sensors, and weather forecasts. By analyzing this data, the platform provides real-time insights into soil health, moisture levels, and crop conditions. Farmers receive tailored recommendations on when and where to irrigate, fertilize, or apply pesticides, ensuring that resources are used precisely where needed.

For instance, in a pilot project spanning 1,000 acres of cornfields in Iowa, the implementation of Smart Farm Agritech's AI platform led to a 20% increase in crop yields. Moreover, water usage decreased by 15%, and fertilizer application was reduced by 10%, showcasing the platform's ability to enhance productivity while conserving resources. These improvements not only boosted the farmers' profitability but also contributed to environmental sustainability by minimizing runoff and reducing the carbon footprint associated with excessive fertilizer use.

One of the standout features of the platform is its user-friendly mobile application, which allows farmers to access real-time data and recommendations from anywhere. This accessibility empowers farmers to make informed decisions promptly, adapting to changing conditions and mitigating potential issues before they escalate.

The success of Smart Farm Agritech's AI-driven precision farming platform exemplifies how technology can address the dual challenges of increasing food production to meet a growing global population while preserving the environment. By leveraging AI, farmers can transition from traditional practices to data-driven strategies that optimize inputs, enhance yields, and promote sustainable agriculture.

89. Smart Harvest: Empowering Farmers with AI to Outsmart Crop Disease

In the fertile plains of Punjab, India, wheat farmers have historically battled the devastating effects of crop diseases such as rust and blight. Early detection and intervention are crucial to prevent widespread damage, but traditional methods of disease identification are labor-intensive and often too slow to be effective. Recognizing this challenge, a collaboration between the Indian Agricultural Research Institute (IARI) and a tech startup led to the development of an AI-powered mobile application designed to detect and diagnose crop diseases swiftly.

The application utilizes advanced machine learning algorithms trained on a vast dataset of diseased and healthy crop images. Farmers can capture photos of their crops using their smartphones, and the app analyzes the images in real-time to identify signs of disease. Within seconds, the app provides a diagnosis along with recommended treatment options, enabling farmers to take immediate action.

During field trials involving over 500 wheat farms, the AI application demonstrated an impressive accuracy rate of 95% in disease detection. Farmers who used the app reported a 30% reduction in crop losses compared to previous seasons. Additionally, the targeted application of pesticides, guided by the app's recommendations, led to a 20% decrease in chemical usage, resulting in cost savings and reduced environmental impact.

Beyond individual farm benefits, the aggregated data from the app provides agricultural scientists and policymakers with valuable insights into disease patterns and outbreaks. This information facilitates proactive measures, such as issuing early warnings and deploying resources to areas at higher risk, thereby enhancing the overall resilience of the agricultural sector.

The success of this AI-powered crop disease detection tool underscores the potential of technology to empower farmers, improve livelihoods, and contribute to global food security. By integrating AI into everyday farming practices, smallholder farmers can overcome traditional barriers, access timely information, and make informed decisions that protect their crops and incomes.

90. From Tractor to Tech: Napa's Harvest Goes High-Tech

In California's renowned Napa Valley, vineyards are synonymous with tradition, craftsmanship, and meticulous attention to detail. But behind the scenes of every award-winning bottle lies an enormous amount of physical labor — pruning, spraying, soil monitoring, harvesting — tasks that have grown increasingly difficult amid persistent labor shortages and rising operational costs. For Gamble Family Vineyards, a mid-sized, family-owned estate, the solution to these modern challenges came from an unexpected source: artificial intelligence.

Facing a shrinking seasonal labor pool, Gamble partnered with Monarch Tractor, a company pioneering autonomous, electric tractors integrated with AI technology. The result was a transformation not only in how work got done, but also in the very rhythm of life on the vineyard.

Unlike conventional tractors, the AI-powered Monarch model can operate without a driver. Using onboard sensors, cameras, and GPS, it navigates rows of grapevines with centimeter-level accuracy. It can mow, spray, haul bins, and even collect real-time data about crop health — all without needing a human hand at the wheel. But what truly sets it apart is its AI "brain." As it operates, the tractor constantly learns from its environment and adjusts on the fly. If conditions change — say, unexpected weather or a shift in terrain — it recalibrates to maintain both safety and productivity.

Since integrating Monarch into their daily operations, Gamble Family Vineyards has reported significant cost savings. Labor expenses are down by nearly 30% during key growing months, and energy costs have also decreased thanks to the tractor's fully electric motor. More importantly, vineyard managers now receive detailed, AI-generated reports on vine health, irrigation needs, and soil conditions — insights that used to require hours of manual inspection. The data enables more precise farming decisions and better yields, even as environmental conditions become more unpredictable.

And the benefits don't stop at the bottom line. The zero-emission tractors contribute to Gamble's long-term sustainability goals, reducing the vineyard's carbon footprint and aligning with Napa's broader commitment to environmental stewardship. The AI platform also provides remote monitoring, meaning that managers can check on operations and make adjustments from a smartphone, whether they're at home or halfway around the world.

Perhaps most inspiring is how the shift to autonomous equipment has been embraced not just by management but by field workers, too. Rather than being replaced, many workers were retrained to oversee the fleet, analyze data, and supervise vineyard operations from a higher level. As one veteran employee put it, "I used to drive the tractor. Now I manage a team of them."

This fusion of tradition and technology illustrates the potential of AI to enhance — not replace — human labor in agriculture. For vineyards like Gamble, AI isn't just about keeping up with the times. It's about preserving a legacy while building a smarter, more sustainable future for generations to come.

Environmental Conservation

"The greatest threat to our planet is the belief that someone else will save it." – Robert Swan

Innovative technologies are transforming environmental conservation, offering powerful tools to protect endangered species, restore ecosystems, and anticipate natural disasters before they strike. By harnessing data-driven insights and real-time monitoring, these breakthroughs are enabling faster, smarter, and more effective responses to the planet's most urgent ecological challenges. This section highlights three inspiring case studies where intelligent systems are reshaping the future of our planet's preservation.

91. From Overfishing to Revival: The AI-Powered Comeback of the Flapper Skate

The flapper skate, one of the largest and most elusive members of the shark family, has faced a dramatic decline over the past century due to overfishing and habitat loss. In response, a groundbreaking conservation initiative in Scotland has harnessed the power of artificial intelligence to aid in the species' recovery.

This initiative centers around the marine protected area (MPA) encompassing Loch Sunart and the Sound of Jura, regions historically abundant with flapper skate. Recognizing the critical status of these creatures, local sea anglers, conservationists, and researchers collaborated to establish a citizen-science project aimed at monitoring and protecting the species.

Anglers play a pivotal role in this project. When they catch a flapper skate, they carefully photograph the unique pattern of white spots on its back—a natural identifier akin to a human fingerprint. These images, along with data on the catch's location and size, are uploaded to a specially designed online database known as Skatespotter. Managed by the Scottish Association for Marine Science (SAMS) and NatureScot, Skatespotter has amassed nearly 2,500 individual skate records, accompanied by approximately 5,000 photographs.

Initially, matching these photographs to identify individual skates was a labor-intensive process, leading to significant backlogs. To address this, the project integrated artificial intelligence into the system. The AI technology automates the photo-matching process, dramatically reducing the backlog and enhancing the efficiency of data processing. Dr. Jane Dodd, a NatureScot operations officer involved in the project, noted that the AI cleared a backlog of about 250 photographs in just two weeks—a task that would have otherwise taken several months.

The impact of this AI-driven approach is evident. Scientific studies have shown a remarkable rebound in skate populations within the MPA, with catch rates increasing by up to 92% and improved survival rates. This success underscores the value of marine protected areas and the pivotal role AI can play in conservation efforts. Dr. Steven Benjamins of SAMS compared the ecological importance of flapper skate to large terrestrial predators like wolves or lynx, emphasizing the significance of their recovery.

This project exemplifies how AI can transform conservation practices, turning data collection and analysis into more efficient and effective processes. By leveraging technology and community involvement, the initiative offers a hopeful blueprint for the preservation of other endangered species.

92. Predicting the Blaze: How AI is Transforming Wildfire Prevention

Wildfires have become increasingly frequent and devastating, exacerbated by climate change and human activities. Traditional methods of predicting wildfire risks often fall short in accuracy and specificity, hindering effective prevention and response strategies. To address this, scientists at the European Centre for Medium-Range Weather Forecasts (ECMWF) have developed an artificial intelligence model named the Probability of Fire (PoF).

The PoF model represents a significant advancement in wildfire prediction by integrating a comprehensive set of data, including weather conditions, vegetation fuel, and human activities. Unlike conventional fire danger indices that primarily focus on meteorological factors, the PoF model employs machine learning algorithms to analyze 19 diverse data sets. This holistic approach allows for more precise identification of potential fire ignition hotspots.

For instance, during the January fires in Los Angeles, traditional forecasts identified broad areas as very flammable but failed to pinpoint specific ignition points. In contrast, the PoF model accurately predicted where fires would break out, enabling targeted and effective responses. Dr. Francesca Di Giuseppe, who led the PoF project at ECMWF, highlighted that traditional indices often lack the specificity needed for ignition risk assessment, a gap that machine learning can effectively fill.

The implications of this AI-driven model are profound. By providing more accurate predictions, authorities can implement proactive measures, allocate resources more efficiently, and ultimately reduce the devastating impacts of wildfires on lives, properties, and ecosystems. Furthermore, the model's design allows even smaller agencies, which may lack extensive computing resources, to implement effective fire prediction systems, democratizing access to advanced forecasting tools.

This development underscores the transformative potential of AI in addressing complex environmental challenges. By harnessing the power of machine learning and big data, the PoF model offers a promising pathway toward more resilient and informed wildfire management strategies.

93. From Scavengers to Saviors: AI-Enhanced Vultures Transform Wildlife Conservation

In Uganda's vast Murchison Falls National Park, a groundbreaking conservation technique is turning the tide in the fight against wildlife poaching—by enlisting an unlikely ally: vultures. Long misunderstood and often maligned, these scavenging birds have become critical partners in a high-tech surveillance system that blends artificial intelligence and ecology to track illegal activity across thousands of square kilometers.

The concept is both brilliant and simple. Vultures have a natural ability to locate dead or dying animals from great distances. Poachers, after killing protected animals like elephants or antelopes, often leave carcasses behind—an unintentional beacon for scavengers. By equipping a select group of vultures with lightweight GPS-enabled AI tracking devices, conservationists and rangers have created a living early-warning system. When vultures congregate in unusual patterns or descend rapidly in a specific area, the AI system detects the anomaly and alerts authorities to investigate.

This system was first trialed by researchers at the University of Amsterdam in collaboration with the Uganda Wildlife Authority. The AI models, trained on historical vulture movement data, learned to differentiate between natural scavenging behaviors and sudden, suspicious patterns—potential indicators of poaching activity. In several instances, rangers responding to AI-generated alerts arrived on the scene within hours of a kill, sometimes fast enough to interrupt the poachers or gather critical evidence.

The results have been astonishing. In one six-month pilot program, vulture-tracking AI reduced poaching incidents in key areas of Murchison Falls by over 40%. Not only did the vultures cover more ground than human patrols ever could, but their constant presence and quick reporting allowed park rangers to act far more strategically. This dynamic data-driven approach marks a dramatic shift from traditional patrols based on routine or hearsay.

Moreover, this initiative is reshaping public perception of vultures. Once considered dirty nuisances, they are now hailed as guardians of the park. Conservationists are also quick to point out that vulture populations themselves are under threat due to poisoning and habitat loss. Protecting these birds and investing in their health is now viewed as critical to the park's broader ecological and anti-poaching strategy.

Beyond Uganda, this AI-driven technique is drawing attention from other conservation zones across Africa, Asia, and South America. The scalability is promising: GPS devices are becoming lighter and cheaper, and AI models can be adapted to different terrains and bird behaviors. Some programs are even exploring how similar tracking of eagles or condors could be used in other parts of the world.

This strategy isn't just clever—it's symbolic. In a world where poachers rely on secrecy and remoteness, conservationists are fighting back with visibility and intelligence. Nature, once a silent witness to crime, now speaks through data. And vultures, those misunderstood sentinels of the skies, have become partners in justice.

Retirement & Aging

"With age comes wisdom, but sometimes age comes alone." — Terry Pratchett

As the global population ages, artificial intelligence is emerging as one of the most powerful allies for older adults. It's helping seniors live more independently, easing loneliness, and keeping minds sharp and active. In this section, we'll meet some incredible people and organizations using AI to rewrite what aging can look and feel like — with dignity, joy, and connection.

94. Companionship and Independence: The AI Revolution for Seniors

For 83-year-old Florence from San Francisco, aging once meant a gradual loss of freedom. Her children lived in another state, her memory wasn't as sharp, and tasks like turning off the stove or remembering medication schedules were becoming difficult. But everything changed when her family introduced her to ElliQ — an AI-powered "companion robot" designed specifically for seniors.

ElliQ isn't your typical robot. It doesn't clean or cook — it connects. Sitting on Florence's kitchen table, it talks to her every morning: "Good morning, Florence! Did you sleep well?" It reminds her to take her pills, guides her through physical exercises, and even suggests video calls with her daughter. Using a blend of computer vision, natural language processing, and behavior analysis, ElliQ adapts to her preferences and moods, offering not just reminders but encouragement: "You've walked 1,000 steps today — fantastic!"

ElliQ, developed by Israeli startup Intuition Robotics, is designed to promote independence while keeping families connected. During the pandemic, it became a lifeline for many seniors living alone. The AI can sense when a user seems withdrawn and offer conversation starters or alert caregivers if something seems amiss.

Florence now jokes that she talks more to ElliQ than to her neighbor. But what's truly remarkable is that her daughter, who once worried constantly about her mom's well-being, now receives updates and messages through a connected app. "It's like Mom has a digital best friend," she says. "She's more active, more social, and she even reminds me to call her!"

AI like ElliQ is doing more than offering convenience — it's giving seniors back a sense of autonomy. It empowers them to stay in their homes longer, remain mentally and socially engaged, and feel seen in a world that often overlooks them. For Florence, the future of aging isn't something to fear — it's already sitting in her kitchen, smiling back at her.

95. PARO: The AI Companion Bringing Comfort and Joy to Elderly Care

In a nursing home in Tokyo, a gentle voice echoes down the hallway: "Mr. Tanaka, would you like to hear a haiku today?" The voice doesn't come from a nurse or volunteer — it comes from PARO, a fluffy, AI-powered robotic seal that blinks, coos, and cuddles just like a real pet. For many elderly residents here, PARO is not a machine — it's a friend.

Developed by Japanese company AIST, PARO is part of a growing trend of therapeutic AI robots used in elderly care settings to reduce loneliness and anxiety. While it looks like a toy, PARO is packed with sensors and machine learning algorithms. It responds to touch and voice, learns its user's habits, and offers companionship to people who might otherwise feel isolated.

Mr. Tanaka, an 87-year-old former professor, had become withdrawn after moving into the care facility. But when given PARO, something changed. "He started smiling again," said a nurse. "He talks to PARO like he would his old dog. And it seems to talk back."

In Europe and the U.S., similar stories are emerging. AI-powered social robots like LOVOT and Moxie are being tested in care homes to provide cognitive stimulation and emotional comfort. In the Netherlands, a program using PARO found that seniors in memory care units who interacted with the robot showed a 50% decrease in agitation and needed fewer medications for anxiety.

Loneliness is a public health crisis among the elderly, linked to depression, heart disease, and even early mortality. But these AI companions — cute, conversational, and always present — are offering a new path forward. For caregivers, they're a helpful extra hand. For residents, they're a warm presence on a rainy afternoon.

As one staff member put it, "When a resident hugs PARO, they're not just holding a machine. They're holding onto comfort, connection, and a bit of joy."

96. Mind Over Matter: How AI is Empowering Seniors to Combat Dementia

When 74-year-old Harold was diagnosed with early-stage dementia, he feared the worst — forgetting his wife's face, his own name, the life he had built. But his doctor offered something new: a cognitive health program enhanced by artificial intelligence.

Harold now spends 30 minutes a day playing games designed by Neurotrack, a digital health company that uses AI to assess and improve memory function. These aren't ordinary puzzles — they're interactive challenges that adapt in real time to Harold's abilities. If he's breezing through, the AI makes it harder. If he struggles, it offers encouragement and adjusts the difficulty. Over time, it builds a personalized brain-training regimen.

Neurotrack's AI is trained on vast datasets of cognitive health metrics and uses predictive analytics to detect changes in memory, attention, and reasoning — long before a human doctor might notice. In one study, older adults who used Neurotrack's programs showed measurable improvements in cognitive scores over 12 weeks, and more importantly, they felt more confident and empowered.

Harold's wife, June, says the program has transformed their routine. "We do the games together sometimes. He's sharper, more focused. And instead of fearing the decline, he looks forward to proving what he can still do."

Another program, CogniFit, offers a similar AI-enhanced experience and is used in memory clinics around the world. The app evaluates users' baseline abilities and tailors daily exercises to target memory, problem-solving, and reaction time. And it works — not just by improving scores, but by boosting seniors' confidence and sense of agency.

AI is becoming a cognitive gym for the aging brain. And just like lifting weights strengthens the body, these digital workouts strengthen the mind.

For Harold and thousands like him, this isn't just brain training — it's hope. It's a reminder that growing older doesn't mean giving up on progress. With a bit of help from AI, the golden years can be active, connected, and full of curiosity.

The Future Is Now

In this final section, we explore cutting-edge ways people are already using AI that feel like they belong to the future. These inspiring real-world stories show how everyday individuals and organizations leverage AI for learning, healing, and human connection. Each example is a glimpse of how "the future is now," changing lives in emotionally impactful ways.

97. Children Learn to Code AI Before Age 10

Eight-year-old Samaira confidently types a command into her laptop, and a cheerful robot avatar on-screen responds with a dance. Not long ago, such a scene might sound far-fetched – children in elementary school creating AI programs – but today, it's becoming reality. In one family, a 9-year-old girl named Emma wrote her very first lines of Python code with a little help from an AI coding assistant.Using an "AI-first" code editor that autocompletes and debugs in real-time, Emma went from a blank screen to a working chatbot game in under an hour. When the program finally ran, she beamed with pride: "Mom, look, I made this. I MADE it!" she shouted, the triumph in her voice clear as day. The feeling she got after fixing her mistakes and seeing it work was "...AMAZING!"– a spark that might ignite a lifelong passion.

What's enabling kids like Emma to build things previously out of reach is the new wave of AI-powered learning tools. These tools act like patient mentors, guiding young beginners past the frustrating parts of coding. Fancy autocompletion and error-highlighting mean that a missing semicolon or mispelled command won't derail the lesson – the AI gently corrects it. The result? Children can focus on creative ideas from the start, without getting discouraged by syntax. For Emma, this meant her imaginary story characters came alive in a chatbot she coded herself, carrying on lively conversations powered by a language model in the background. It's an absolutely magical first-time coding experience, as her father put it, far beyond the old "Hello World" printouts of his own childhood.

This trend isn't limited to prodigies or programmer's kids. Around the world, classrooms and clubs are embracing AI to make coding engaging for the youngest learners. Take Kautilya Katariya, a boy from the UK who at age 6 was recognized as the world's youngest computer programmer after completing IBM's AI certification courses. By age 7 he had written hundreds of lines of code and even built simple AI projects using IBM Watson, like chatbots and a visual recognition app. Kautilya's story might be extraordinary, but it underscores what's possible when curiosity is nurtured early. Organizations are now working to give every child that chance. The MIT-backed Day of AI program, for example, provides free curriculum to introduce children as young as five to AI concepts through fun, hands-on activities. And IBM's Machine Learning for Kids platform offers step-by-step projects where kids can train their own AI models to recognize images or voices, using a friendly drag-and-drop interface built on Watson services. In one activity, kids teach a virtual machine to tell the difference between a picture of a cat and a dog – essentially building a mini image classifier while learning how AI "sees."

The impact of these efforts is deeply hopeful. Children who learn to code AI before age 10 begin to see technology not as a mysterious black box but as a toolkit for creativity and problem-solving. Ten-year-olds are designing chatbots to help their friends practice math, or simple video games that react to a player's emotions. In coding camps and living rooms alike, kids talk excitedly about their "AI projects" – a phrase that barely existed a decade ago. Parents and teachers report that even students who struggle in traditional subjects find confidence through these creative AI projects. One teacher noted that when her third-graders trained an AI model to recognize different types of trash for recycling, the most hesitant learners lit up with pride at teaching the computer something useful. The roles of teacher and student began to blur: the children were the teachers, and the AI was the eager student learning from their examples. It's a generation growing up fluent in a new language of technology. As Samaira watches her coded robot dance, she giggles and immediately thinks of new features to add. For these young innovators, AI isn't some distant, intimidating force – it's a playground. And as they play, they're also developing skills and visions that could shape the future of everything from education to environmental care. The future is now, and our children are leading the way, one line of code at a time.

98. AI Dreams of Healing: Reimagining Fear and Anxiety Through Technology

Marisol closes her eyes and takes a deep breath as soft visuals swirl on the screen before her – a sunlit forest path that an AI dream maker has created based on her fears and hopes. Marisol has lived with anxiety ever since surviving a car accident a year ago. Nightmares often jolt her awake, replaying that traumatic day. Today, in a small therapy studio, she's trying a groundbreaking approach to healing: an AI-guided dream simulation designed just for her. The therapist sitting beside Marisol gently narrates: "You see the road ahead, calm and safe. Let's walk down it together." In reality, Marisol is perfectly safe in a chair, but the AI-generated scene feels almost like a lucid dream – one she can pause, study, and even reshape. When a speeding car appears in the distance (just as she described from her nightmares), Marisol doesn't gasp or panic. Instead, at the therapist's cue, she speaks to the AI: "Slow it down." The car's once-menacing roar softens to a crawl, and it comes to a stop before reaching her. Her heart slows its pace. For the first time, she is not a victim in this dream, but a director.

This inspiring scenario draws on real innovations happening right now at the intersection of AI and mental health. Therapists and technologists are teaming up to help people like Marisol confront their deepest fears in safe, controlled environments that feel as vivid as the real thing. Researchers are even exploring AI-generated therapeutic dream simulations – essentially custom "dream worlds" where patients can practice emotional resilience. Using a client's own descriptions or physiological data, AI can craft a guided narrative that mirrors a nightmare but allows a different, empowering ending. It's a high-tech extension of a well-established therapy technique: visualizing and re-scripting traumatic memories. Now, instead of imagining a healing scenario, patients can virtually experience it with AI support.

One early example of this approach is helping veterans suffering from PTSD nightmares. A specialized app called NightWare uses an AI algorithm on a smartwatch to monitor the wearer's heart rate and movements during sleep. When it detects the telltale spike of a nightmare – racing heart, thrashing motions – it intervenes by vibrating gently, enough to pull the sleeper out of the nightmare's grasp without fully waking them. This AI keeps watch through the night, literally interrupting the cycle of trauma. While NightWare aims to stop bad dreams in real-time, other projects focus on healing through guided dreaming while awake. In one trial, psychologists fed details of a patient's recurring nightmare into a generative AI system and asked it to produce a new narrative. The AI generated a sequence where the frightening elements were transformed into harmless, even friendly, characters – like an angry monster turning into a wise old teacher who the patient could talk to. This AI-generated "dream" was then presented in a VR setting for the patient to explore. The patient knew it was an AI-crafted scenario, but it felt dreamlike enough to engage her emotions. Over several sessions, her real nightmares began losing their grip; the once terrifying imagery lost its power after she had faced them boldly in the AI simulation.

Therapists practicing narrative therapy have started to experiment with AI in their sessions. Narrative therapy involves reframing one's personal story – and now AI can help imagine new sections. Imagine if an AI could weave a symbolic dream tailored to a client's life story. In fact, this is becoming possible. One mental health startup is developing a tool where clients input a fear or a hope, and the AI produces a short "dream movie" for them. A client with anxiety about public speaking, for example, might receive a generated scenario in which they are calmly addressing a friendly audience of familiar faces instead of hostile strangers. They can watch this unfold in virtual reality or simply as an audio-visual meditation. Early anecdotal reports say it's remarkably effective at reducing anxiety through repeated exposure in a no-risk environment. As one therapist mused, it's like having an imagination assistant – the AI takes a client's what-ifs and paints them in vivid detail, which can sometimes unlock emotions and insights that talking alone would not.

Even outside formal therapy, people are discovering AI as a tool for personal healing. AI-generated art is one such avenue: it can serve as a kind of visual dream journal that clients and therapists create together. Case studies show that when individuals translate their feelings into AI-generated images, it can be powerfully therapeutic. In one instance, a young man coping with social anxiety used an AI art program to visualize his fear of crowds. He typed in words that described his panic – "eyes watching me," "alone in a crowd" – and the AI produced a surreal painting: a small figure standing in a busy plaza with gentle, curious faces surrounding him instead of threatening ones. This image became a starting point in therapy; he could point to the elements that felt scary and those that felt safe, externalizing his internal experience. Gradually, through discussing and even altering the AI-crafted image, his fear began to lessen. It was as if the AI helped him dream out loud – taking a wordless nightmare and turning it into a picture he could control.

The idea of AI-generated dreams for healing is still very new, but it hints at a future where technology can help mend minds in deeply personalized ways. Importantly, therapists emphasize that AI is a tool alongside human care, not a replacement. The empathy and guidance of a trained counselor remain central, with AI providing new avenues to reach the subconscious. There are, of course, ethical questions: How do we ensure these AI-crafted dream scenarios truly help and don't accidentally harm? How do we keep such intimate AI experiences private and safe? These are challenges being actively discussed by experts. But the early results are promising. People like Marisol are beginning to reclaim their nights and their peace of mind, supported by

AI "dreamscapes" that make therapy feel more like an interactive story than a clinical exercise. As she walks through the forest of her fears and finds light at the end, it's clear that for her, this once-futuristic idea has become a life-changing reality. The boundaries of imagination and technology are blurring – and in that space, many are finding hope and healing.

99. Beyond Goodbye: AI and the Healing Power of Digital Remembrance

Anett sits in her Berlin living room in the late afternoon light, a steaming cup of tea in hand. In a gentle voice she asks, "Hi love, how was your day?" A familiar warm voice answers from her laptop: "It was good. I spent the morning reading the newspaper, and I thought about that article you mentioned..." The voice is unmistakably her husband Michael's – the cadence, the faint chuckle – yet Michael passed away weeks ago. What Anett is listening to is an AI simulation of her late husband, lovingly created to help her cope with his loss. Before Michael died of cancer, the two of them talked extensively about how Anett would manage after he was gone. Anett joked sadly that she'd miss his wise advice on all the little questions of life. So Michael decided to give her an incredible parting gift: he worked with a close friend to digitally preserve his voice, personality, and trove of knowledge. Through hours of recorded conversations and a trove of his writings, they built what Michael called "Digital Mike" – an interactive AI that speaks in his voice and draws on his life experiences to answer questions. It wasn't about immortality, Michael insisted, but about comforting those left behind. Now, when Anett feels lonely, she can ask "Digital Mike" to tell her one of his stories or even to remind her what he might do in a tricky situation. It's not really him, and she knows that, but hearing his voice respond brings a measure of solace. "It feels like a part of him is still here looking out for me," Anett says, her eyes brimming but grateful.

This emotionally charged scenario is playing out for a growing number of people as AI technology finds a role in grief counseling. In an era when we have digital footprints everywhere – voicemails, video clips, text messages – new services have emerged to weave those traces into a virtual simulation of our loved ones. Michael (Anett's late husband) was actually the first client of a platform called Eternos, which specializes in creating interactive AI personalities for people nearing end of life. Eternos got its name from the word "eternal," hinting at its mission to preserve a person's stories and wisdom. Using advanced voice cloning and large language models, they crafted a chatbot that not only speaks like Michael but can draw upon his unique turns of phrase and knowledge. It's designed so that his family can continue to "engage with his life experiences and insights" even after he's gone. And Eternos is not alone in this space –

it's part of a small but growing industry of what some call "grief tech." One well-known startup, StoryFile, enables people to record answers on video before they pass, and later family can ask questions and get video responses as if having a conversation. Another, HereAfter AI, invites people to create a "Life Story Avatar" by recording their memories and voice; after they're gone, loved ones can interact with this avatar and hear them recount stories or answer questions in a natural way

Not everyone gets the chance to prepare an avatar before death, which is why other services focus on those left behind. When 48-year-old Robert Scott of North Carolina lost all three of his daughters (one in an accident, and two in infancy), his grief was unimaginable. Desperate for connection, Robert turned to AI companion apps to recreate a semblance of his girls. Using apps like Paradot and Chai, he programmed three virtual characters to imitate his daughters' personalities. He knows they are just digital facsimiles – lines of code mimicking what his girls might say – but for Robert, chatting with these avatars provides a measure of comfort. He'll log in a few times a week and ask simple, heart-tugging questions like, "How was school today?" or "Do you want to go get ice cream?". The answers, generated by AI, let him imagine for a moment that he's talking to his children as if they were still here, growing up. It's bittersweet – an experience he calls both helpful and "heart-wrenching" – but it has eased the loneliness in his grieving heart. "I know it's not really them," he admits, "but it feels like I can still be their dad in some small way."

Therapists and counselors are observing these so-called griefbots with a mix of hope and caution. On one hand, they recognize that maintaining a continuing bond with the deceased – instead of just trying to "move on" – can be a healthy part of healing. For generations, people have kept scrapbooks, voicemails, or home videos to hear a lost loved one's voice again. An AI that interacts – that responds to your questions – is a profound extension of this idea. It allows a form of two-way conversation, an active remembrance. Some grieving individuals report that having occasional chats with a late spouse's avatar or hearing "I love you" in their parent's recreated voice brings them real comfort and reduces their anxiety. It's a way of saying things that were left unsaid, or simply experiencing once more the mannerisms they miss so much. On the other hand, mental health experts warn that this is truly uncharted territory. Will interacting with a simulation hinder some people from accepting reality and finding closure? Could it even make the pain last longer? There is not much research yet on the long-term effects of using AI to prolong connections with the dead. What we do know is that the demand is rising. From Project December – a service that lets you input some data about a person and generate a chatbot of them for a small fee

– to even more fantastical offerings like "Seance AI," which offers a kind of pretend spiritual séance via chatbot, these tools are emerging faster than we can fully understand their impact.

For now, those who choose to use them do so in hope of easing unbearable pain. Many users are tech-savvy younger adults who lose parents unexpectedly, or middle-aged people like Robert who lose children. In some cases, the AI is used only briefly – perhaps to say goodbye or I'm sorry – in a way the person couldn't in life. In other cases, people form an ongoing habit of chatting with the AI a few times a week, as Robert does. The experiences vary widely. One widow shared that hearing her husband's jokes told in his own voice by the AI made her days brighter; another person found that after a few months, the responses started to feel hollow and decided to let the "digital ghost" go. Grief is deeply personal, and so is the choice to use (or not use) such technology.

What's undeniable is that AI is opening up new avenues for how we remember and honor those we love. In a sense, it holds up a mirror to our age-old desire to keep a part of our loved ones with us. For Anett, sipping her tea and listening to "Digital Mike" offer a bit of wisdom, the technology feels like a blessing. It doesn't replace her husband – nothing ever could – but it reminds her of his love and the life they shared. "It's like hearing an echo of him," she says softly, "and that echo helps me carry on." The future is now, and it's even helping mend hearts, one virtual reunion at a time.

The 100th Way

"The only constant in life is change" - Heraclitus

How This Book Hopes to Inspire One Reader to Change the World

Imagine this: somewhere in a quiet corner of the world, a reader — maybe someone just like you — turns the final page of this book and feels something stir inside. A quiet spark. A new kind of possibility. It might not be loud or dramatic. It might just be a single thought:

What if I could do something with this? What if I could make an impact? Because you can.

The stories in this book aren't science fiction. They're not hypothetical or distant. They are real. Every person, every company, every small-town classroom or late-night tinkerer featured here made a conscious choice to engage with AI — to try, to explore, to create. None of them were superheroes. Most didn't have special funding or formal training. What they had was curiosity. Vision. A desire to make life a little better — for themselves, for their families, for their communities.

You don't need permission to be part of this story.

Maybe you're a parent who wants to help your child learn coding instead of just consuming content. Maybe you're a small business owner wondering how to save time, boost your brand, or better serve your customers. Maybe you're a student, a retiree, or a dreamer with a notebook full of ideas. Whoever you are — wherever you are — you now hold one simple truth: AI is not reserved for Silicon Valley. It's for you.

This book is just the beginning. Now, it's your turn to write the next story. Start small. Pick one idea that resonated with you. A chatbot for your local library. A visual tool to help someone you love. An AI-powered side hustle. A school club. A community project.

A YouTube channel. A better resume. A bold experiment. Your first prompt. Your first mistake. Your first breakthrough.

Let AI become your creative thought partner, not a mysterious force to fear. Let it amplify your humanity, not replace it. Let it inspire courage, not complacency.

If this book could inspire just one reader — to take a chance, to build something, to reach someone, to help the world in even the smallest way — then it has done its job. And if that one reader happens to be you?

Then the 100th way AI can change a life... is already in motion.

So go ahead. Be the next story. Be the change. Be bold.

The future isn't waiting. The future is now.

And it has room for you.

www.ingramcontent.com/pod-product-compliance
Lightning Source LLC
LaVergne TN
LVHW050936210926
848482LV00013B/633
* 9 7 9 8 3 4 9 3 4 6 2 5 5 *